THE GORGEOUS MASK: DUBLIN 1700 - 1850

Chris Evans

Dublin, March 1990.

THE GORGEOUS MASK:

DUBLIN 1700 - 1850

Edited by
DAVID DICKSON

DUBLIN
TRINITY HISTORY WORKSHOP
1987

Trinity History Workshop

Publication 2

Published 1987

Trinity History Workshop
New Arts Building
Trinity College
Dublin 2

Setting by Trinity History Workshop
Printed by Screen Arts (Ireland), Ltd., Drimnagh Valley, Dublin

ISBN   0 9511400 2 7 (hardback)
         0 9511400 3 5 (softback)
ISSN   0 0790-7087

Contents

Maps

Illustrations

Figures and Tables

INTRODUCTION

It is still the conventional wisdom that the eighteenth century - or at least the last twenty years of it - was a golden age for Dublin. Like most historical half-truths, this myth disguises a far more complex reality. Dublin two centuries ago was indeed visually impressive by west European standards, with its central places newly built or in the process of being re-modelled according to the latest canons of international architectural taste. However writer after writer through the eighteenth century contrasted this civic brilliance with the context within which it was being created: in Swift's generation the contrast had usually been made between the wealth and splendour of the capital, and the rural poverty and 'unimproved' landscapes visible from the main roads that radiated from the city. By the late eighteenth century however, the contrast more often chosen was that between upper-class Dublin, socially and architecturally, and the Neapolitan squalor of the poorer quarters, with their teeming hordes of beggars on every street.

The eighteenth-century city was by any reckoning an expanding one. Yet the very scale of its growth (from about 60,000 residents in 1700 to 224,000 in 1821) cannot be explained without reference to the specific social system of which it was a part: eighteenth-century Dublin's big-spending elite were not its merchants (as had been the case in the seventeenth century) nor its lawyers, its brewers or its distillers (as was to be the case in the nineteenth century), but the owners of rural estates who spent part or all of the year in the capital; their disposable income remained remarkably buoyant for several generations, thanks to a property system which guaranteed landowners a fat share of their tenant-farmers' earnings. Thus although eighteenth-century Ireland experienced considerable economic growth, it remained a profoundly unequal society. Dublin reflected this much more than the provincial cities, not only because it was to there that the very wealthy gravitated, but because the city's commerce (with the notable exception of linen) centred on a number of *import* trades - wine, sugar, fine cloth etc. - and Dublin's wholesale merchants were in the first instance catering for the landed gentry, those most able to afford foreign luxuries, whether they resided in Dublin itself or far inland. The kaleidoscopic variety of specialist craftsmen and artisans who drew a living in Dublin were also profoundly dependant on the continued purchasing power of the landed class.

At the high noon of Dublin's supposed golden age, the 1780s and 1790s, two independent processes, rural population growth and technical changes in manufacturing, were having insidious effects on the capital; together they exacerbated the problem of urban poverty by increasing the immigration of rural labourers and by undermining the earning power of skilled artisans. Unprecedented overcrowding was evident by the 1790s in the oldest city parishes. The well-to-do could tolerate the selective deterioration of the urban environment because they were not part of it. Where not long before aristocrats and master-butchers had shared Smithfield addresses, now such neighbourhoods were being totally deserted by the rich. The old pattern familiar in most pre-industrial cities of the intermixing of high-quality and low-status housing, of new streets and old thoroughfares, of 'town-houses' and bawdy-houses, was now being replaced by spatial segregation within the city. Broadly speaking, the western and older parishes were now bereft of upper-class and wealthier commercial households, the large houses there being sub-divided and let, floor by floor or room by room, to whole families of lodgers, whereas the eastern parishes, some only established since the mid-century, had much lower population densities, open spaces, few artisans and little of the noxious pollution that scarred the poorer areas.

The architectural legacy of 'Georgian Dublin' is, with few exceptions, sited in what was in 1800 the eastern half of the city. The Liberties in the south-west of the old town have been completely rebuilt (in some parts twice rebuilt) since 1800, and the oldest city parishes are now depopulated, draughty reminders of the failure of twentieth-century city planners. But even the battered legacy of the east, the linear streetscapes, the classical facades and the leafy squares, are a misleading guide to the urban environment within which they were constructed. For all of Dublin in its eighteenth-century phase of rapid growth was contained within what by modern standards was a claustrophobically small urban site. Late twentieth-century Greater Dublin may be more than four times as populous as the city *circa* 1800, but it is spread over an area perhaps twenty times as large. All cities before the railway, the telegraph and the internal combustion engine had to be much more tightly knit, but Dublin was particularly congested and unplanned because of its rapid rate of growth and the limited control that public bodies had had over its physical development. The Wide Streets Commissioners were beginning to replan its central street system in the 1780s, but their success was still only partial when they were dissolved sixty years later.

The essays here explore one polarity in this tale of contrasts. The coexistence of great wealth and great poverty within the pressurised capsule of the metropolis seems to have made more visible certain traits implicit in Irish society at large. It demonstrated the uses and abuses of wealth, and the energetic, individualistic and ultimately imperfect responses of the propertied classes to perceived social problems - destitution, petty crime, business failure. Dublin was both laboratory and hot-house, example and warning.

*   *   *

The editorial board of the Workshop would like to extend their gratitude to the myriad of persons and groups without whose help the idea behind this volume could never have become reality. Financial aid came from C.B.T. Systems, Upper Mount Street, Dublin; the Rohan Group, Mount Street Crescent, Dublin; Pilkington Glass, Merrion Square, Dublin; Unilever Management Services, Harcourt Centre, Dublin; Bank of Ireland, College Green, Dublin; Coca-Cola, Western Industrial Estate, Dublin; the Grace Lawless Lee Fund, Trinity College; the Management Committee of Irish Historical Studies and the CSC Publications Committee, Trinity College.We would also like to extend our special thanks to the Trinity Trust for their continued support over the last two years.

We are grateful to the following institutions for permission to quote from manuscripts in their possession: The British Library; Marsh's Library (Dublin); Public Record Office (Dublin); Public Record Office of Northern Ireland (Belfast); Representative Church Body (C. of I.) Library (Dublin); Royal Dublin Society; and Trinity College Dublin. We are also grateful to the British Library for permission to publish the illustration on p.35 and to the Royal Society of Antiquaries of Ireland for permission to publish that on p.163.

The individuals who lent us their assistance, and who sometimes saved us from disaster, are almost too numerous to recall. Particular thanks must go to Professor Aidan Clarke and Muriel Saidlear of the Department of Modern History, Trinity College; Dr. Patrick Kelly, Vivien Jenkins, Margaret Lawlor and Olive Murtagh of the Arts (Humanities) Faculty, Trinity College; Professor Brian Boydell; Michael Doherty, Jim Laraghy, Maire McAnally and all the staff of the Computer Laboratory, Trinity College; Noel Mooney of Mooney's Art Machine; Gary O' Callaghan of the Computing Workshop, Lombard St., for his invaluable technical assistance; Mrs. M. Lyons for drawing the figures; Peter Mooney and his colleagues on the Security Staff, and the attendants in the Arts Block, Trinity College; and finally to all the members of the current Workshop: Imelda Brophy, Bernadette Doorley, Margaret Downes, Richard English, David Fitzpatrick, Paul Fitzpatrick, Paul Huggard, Ruth Lavelle, Tighearnan Mooney, David O'Toole, Elizabeth Reddin, and Fiona White.

David Dickson
David Kelly
Deirdre Lindsay
Franc Myles
Joseph O' Carroll
Eamon Walsh

THE GENTRY'S WINTER SEASON

TIGHEARNAN MOONEY
AND
FIONA WHITE

For the landowning classes of eighteenth-century Ireland, Dublin was as obligatory a place to visit as the country fair was to the cattle farmer. Above all, it was the place where they could meet large numbers of their own class on a regular basis in congenial surroundings. Rural life in the big house was often isolated and constricting: Dublin was the essential antidote with its theatre, balls, assemblies, card-parties and concerts, such was the variety of formal and informal modes of upper-class interaction and entertainment in the city. The tastes and fashions of Dublin were themselves derivative - mainly though not exclusively imported from Hanoverian London. However, as a centre for upper-class entertainment and cultural activity, Dublin had the reputation of being second only to London in the English-speaking world.

The presence of wealthy landed families in Dublin fluctuated on a seasonal basis. During the summer there was a noticeable exodus from the city, with better-off people taking holidays or returning to manage their country estates. In early winter the coaches returned to town and the large town-houses filled up again as upper-class social events began to multiply.

The traditional dates of this 'Winter Season' were from November to March. There was also an 'afterseason', a second social peak in late April and May - although it is more difficult

1

to pinpoint this as it differed slightly from year to year. The two quietest months were September and October.

It has often been argued that it was the Irish Parliament and its calendar which determined the number and content of events in the city's winter season, the assumption being that there was a much larger than usual influx of wealthy people into Dublin when Parliament was in session. From 1715 until the 1780s Parliament usually met in Dublin every second winter for five to eight months. However analysis of advertisements for various public entertainments in Dublin newspapers between 1762 and 1765 does not confirm this.[1] The total number of advertisements for plays, assemblies, balls, charity sermons, club meetings and concerts for the 1764 winter season, when Parliament's doors were closed, was in fact higher than the number for the previous winter when Parliament was sitting.[2] It would appear from these figures that a Dublin winter season without a Parliament might actually be more eventful than one with a Parliament. Admittedly this anomaly can be partly accounted for by the fact that during the winter of 1764-65 the Theatre Royal in Crow St. and the Smock Alley theatre were going through a phase of fierce competition, causing great public excitement. When the figures are broken down into separate totals for assemblies, balls, charity sermons and meetings, the result is that there was in fact slightly less going on in Dublin *outside* the purely theatrical sphere during that winter. However, the more important finding is how little difference the sitting of Parliament seems to have had on the number of public events during the season.

A similar analysis of newspaper advertisements in the mid-1780s broadly confirms this pattern. Newspapers are not of course an infallible guide to public events in the city, for there are quite frequent random references to balls and assemblies for which no advertisement was, it seems, placed. Furthermore, by the 1780s, large private balls seem to have been more common.[3] Despite such reservations about the newspaper evidence, it is apparent that in the period 1783-85, the winter season's flow and ebb was not unduly determined by College Green: in 1783-84 the social season more or less corresponded

3

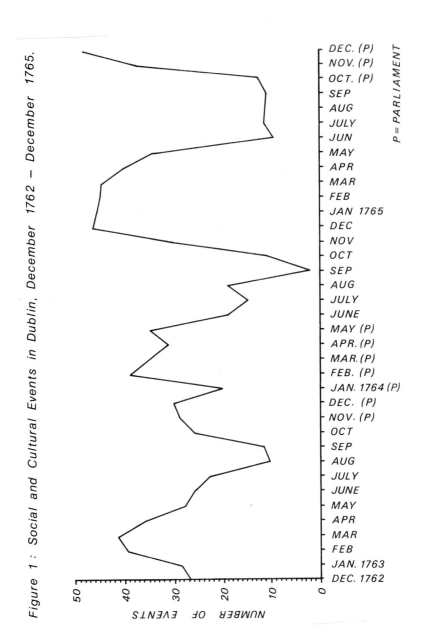

Figure 1 : Social and Cultural Events in Dublin, December 1762 – December 1765.

P = PARLIAMENT

DEC. (P)
NOV. (P)
OCT. (P)
SEP
AUG
JULY
JUN
MAY
APR
MAR
FEB
JAN. 1765
DEC
NOV
OCT
SEP
AUG
JULY
JUNE
MAY (P)
APR. (P)
MAR. (P)
FEB. (P)
JAN. 1764 (P)
DEC. (P)
NOV. (P)
OCT
SEP
AUG
JULY
JUNE
MAY
APR
MAR
FEB
JAN. 1763
DEC. 1762

NUMBER OF EVENTS

50 40 30 20 10 0

with the sitting of Parliament (October 1783-May 1784), but in
the following winter, theatrical activity was broadly similar,
despite the fact that Parliament did not assemble until January
1785. Yet the *Dublin Evening Post* on 15 January 1785
referred to the roads leading into Dublin being

> crowded by a prodigious concourse of nobility and gentry coming to
> Dublin to attend to the business of Parliament, Congress and the
> Courts of Justice.[4]

Was this merely journalistic exaggeration, or was formal entertainment and its market much greater than the demand
generated by parliamentary families? Before answering this,
we need to look closer at the different forms of entertainment
that late eighteenth-century Dublin offered the better-heeled.

*   *   *

Where did people go to be entertained in Dublin during the
latter half of the eighteenth century? Firstly, there was the
theatre. The Theatre Royal in Crow St., the Smock Alley
theatre, and for a short time Stretche's Theatre in Capel St.
which specialised in puppet shows, were the main venues.
Theatrical success was dependent on the patronage of the Lord
Lieutenant and the success of a new play could often depend on
his presence.[5] On occasion Dublin Castle would pay theatres to
perform certain works, sometimes on special dates such as the
king's birthday. This was replaced however at a later stage by
an annual grant of one hundred pounds for the performance of
four plays. These nights were considered to be the most
fashionable of the season.[6] During the 1763-64 season the then
Lord Lieutenant, the Earl of Northumberland, expressed a keen
interest in the theatre and in the first three months of 1764 there
were ten command performances, all in the Theatre Royal.[7]
(This perhaps may go some way to explaining the distinct
absence of reference in the newspapers to the Castle as a centre
for high-society gatherings at the time.)[8]

The theatre in Dublin, perhaps more than any other
entertainment, followed London's fashions. Only a play that
had been successful there would be performed in Dublin.[9] Irish

works were not performed, although some Irish airs were adapted and used as musical interludes (during breaks in a performance).[10] It was not until the last quarter of the century that so-called 'Irish music' began to be popular with Dublin audiences.[11] The managers of Dublin theatres during the summer lull would travel to London to pick up new works and engage performers. In 1761 Henry Mossop, manager of Smock Alley, brought over a company of Italian performers with the intention of staging Italian burlettas. Mossop was attempting to interest the conservative Dublin audiences in a wider range of music where previously English drama and comic or ballad opera had been the staple diet of Dublin theatre-goers. In order to make the Italian burletta seasons more easily accepted Mossop made sure that popular English works diluted the Italian performances.Even then however, they were not very successful. Walsh has argued that one of the main reasons for this was that Irish audiences simply did not like innovation or foreign performers.[12]

The first complete season of Italian opera was not until 1777-78, when performances took place in the Great Musick Hall, Fishamble St. However a great deal of controversy surrounded this new dramatic form during that and the following winters; incidents included press attacks on Carnevale, the organiser of the 1781-82 season, and the hiring of a well-known prostitute called Peg to disturb a number of performances. Rumours of a love affair between one of the Italian singers, Signora Castini, and Henry Grattan added extra spice to the controversy.[13] Italian opera was in fact a failure: Carnevale and his associates lost it seems somewhere in the region of £2,000 in their attempts to broaden the tastes of Dublin audiences.[14]

The most popular kind of theatre entertainment during this period was comic opera; the first successful Dublin production had been 'The Beggar's Opera' in the late 1720s, and it was constantly revived. Shakespeare was also ever popular. Broadly the same mix of plays tended to crop up again and again. In the 1764-65 season 'The Beggar's Opera' was performed 21 times, 'Love in a Village' 15 times, 'The Maid of the Mill' 12 times, 'All in the Wrong' 10 times, 'Artaxerxes' 8 times, and 'Philaster' 8 times.

Audiences were not shy in voicing their opinions of the actors during the performance. The nobility and the ladies sat in the boxes. The 'young gentlemen' were situated in the Pit, which was the area immediately in the front of the orchestra. The servants and trades people sat in the middle and upper galleries. These arrangements were quite strict. For example, if any women appeared in the Pit,

> the whole front row of the upper gallery are suffered to amuse themselves by pelting them with apple skins or orange peel - and still further, their garments are abused by a parcel of ruffians spitting and squirting filth upon them. [15]

Before the Kelly riots of 1747, people were allowed to stand on the stage with the actors while the performance was going on, but by the 1760s the stage and the orchestra were railed off from the audience. Even then the gentlemen of the Pit considered it their duty to upset the performance as much as possible. These anachronistic practices continued in Dublin much longer than in London and may go some way towards explaining why the more serious students of drama in Dublin had by the 1780s retreated into amateur dramatics.

The people of 'high society', more often than not, went to the theatre to flaunt both themselves and their children, all wearing the latest London fashions. In many ways the actual performance took second place to the gossiping and flirting in the audience.[16] The theatres themselves were not very well lit, although accidents with the lighting gave rise to numerous fire alarms; in May 1764 an alarm in the Theatre Royal, Crow St. resulted in a stampede for the exits in which a husband and wife were killed.[17] Accoustics were often quite bad both in theatres and in the concert halls. The ventilation was also frequently poor which brought complaints from summer theatre-goers in particular.[18]

Some element of novelty was essential in theatrical programmes, something 'never seen in this kingdom', or 'completely new scenery, dresses, decorations, etc', 'completely novel'; eighteenth-century theatre managers had to be masters of the art of public relations. Often the novelty was simply an old opera with new music or with just one new air. Tomasso Giordani, one of the most popular composers in Dublin in the late eighteenth century, opened the 'English Opera House' on Capel St. for the season of 1783-84, for which he composed a new opera 'Gibralter' and a comic opera 'The Haunted House'. The English Opera House emphasised in its advertisements the fact that 'something novel' happened every week, although 'Gibralter' ran through the season (23 times) being billed as 'a completely new opera'.[19] Before and after his season in the English Opera House, Giordani worked in other theatres, composing new airs and pieces for various operas. Theatre managers also used other gimmicks to attract audiences, as in the 1784-85 season when Richard Daly brought performing dogs from France to the Theatre Royal, Smock Alley.[20]

An evening at the theatre did not simply consist of one play as it does to-day. The musical element was usually an attraction in itself. If a tragedy was performed, it was usually followed by a ballad or comic opera, singing, instrumental music or a dance. A comic opera could be followed by a farce or 'musical entertainment', a duet, a dance or sometimes a piano concerto. Professional actors and actresses had to be versatile and be able to sing and dance.

Apart from the music performed in the theatre, there were also full concerts. The most frequent venues were churches, particularly St. Patrick's and Christ Church Cathedrals. Large oratorio-type concerts were given there, usually for the benefit of certain charities, notably hospitals. By mid-century one of the most frequently-used musical venues was the Great Musick Hall in Fishamble St. In the winter of 1764-65, there were thirteen Grand Balls advertised, thirteen assemblies, twenty-five concerts and one 'entertainment' sponsored by the Lord Lieutenant.[21] Many of these were benefits for the various charity organisations, for 'distressed weavers' or other specific people in need. All the concerts consisted of works by Handel who was much the most popular composer with Dublin audiences at the time. The Great Musick Hall was rarely used

during the summer: during the whole of the summer of 1765
there were only two morning concerts advertised for the venue.
The Great Assembly Rooms in Brunswick St. were also
very popular. The management specialised in the organisation
of assemblies and balls. There were ten balls and thirteen
assemblies during the 1763-4 season, seven balls during the
parliamentary sessions and seven during the next Parliament-
less winter. The assemblies in the Brunswick St. venue took
place at irregular intervals throughout the period. However, the
Rooms were in decline: between May and December 1765,
only one event, an assembly, was advertised in the papers.[22]

In the 1780s the Grand Ridotto Room and the Exhibition
Room on William St. were fashionable venues for balls and
assemblies. The balls in the Exhibition Room were given by a
variety of promoters, including it seems dance teachers.[23] Mr.
Fontaine gave four 'Cotillion Parties and Suppers' between
February and June in 1784.[24] There were also benefit balls held
in the Exhibition Rooms, such as the one for Miss Ussher on 3
June 1784 which was patronised by the Duchess of Rutland,
the wife of the Lord Lieutenant. The new Gentleman's Clubs
sometimes organised balls, as for example in June 1784 when
the 'Funny Club' of Kildare St. organised two balls for the
benefit of Irish manufacturers. A ball normally consisted of
dancing, supper, tea, negus and sometimes card-playing.

The Rotunda Assembly Rooms were also used to hold balls
during the winter, normally for the benefit of the Lying-In
Hospital. Between February and early April of 1785 and 1786,
there were three such 'Conscription Balls' in the Rotunda.
These were publicly patronised by leading ladies of society,
including both the Duchess of Leinster and Countess Tyrone
(1786), Countess' Moira and Charlemont (1785 and 1786),
Countess Bective (1785) and Mrs La Touche (1785 and
1786).[25]

By the 1780s many leaders of society held musical evenings
in their homes, prominent among these being the first governor
of the Bank of Ireland, David La Touche. In 1787, with a
group of noblemen, he set up the Irish Musical Fund for the
support of 'decayed musicians and their families' They raised

money by subscription and by annual concerts, the first of which was held in commemoration of Handel in St. Werburgh's Church. This was a spectacular affair, involving apparently 300 performers, and was far larger than the oratorio concerts of earlier in the century.[26]

As with theatre, concerts were rarer in summer and early autumn. However in summertime great public musical events were organised outdoors: the 'New Gardens in Great Britain St.' beside the Rotunda were very popular for grand illuminated concerts. These were organised three or four times a month in the mid-1760s. By the 1780s there were Rotunda concerts every Wednesday and Friday and on most Sundays (when the gardens would be illuminated). The summer season in this case ran from April until the beginning of September.[27] Once the season had ended, the various artists who had performed during the summer would hold their own benefit concerts.[28]

On the west side of town the City Basin - before it was transformed by the bustle of the Grand Canal Harbour - was used for summer concerts, accompanied sometimes by fireworks. On the south side of the city beyond the built up area, a Mr. Hollister opened up an imitation of London's 'Ranelagh Gardens' in 1767. It was a great success. During summer evenings the 'beaux and the belles' were to be seen ostentatiously parading themselves there.[29] Gentlemen wore their swords and some even wore stars on their coats to denote their rank. The ladies wore white powder on their faces and fashionable dresses with hoops so wide that hinges were fitted on both sides so that they were able to pass through doorways and enter sedan chairs. Dublin's Ranelagh Gardens were not only an evening location. Formal entertainments were held during the day: at noon on 30 May 1777 there was a Grand Venetian Breakfast followed by a ball.[30] However in the long run, Ranelagh Gardens did not compete successfully against the expanding attractions beside the Rotunda, notably the New Gardens which were opened there in the 1760s.[31]

* * *

Pony Races at the Theatre Royal, Crow St. (*Walker's Hibernian Magazine*, Nov. 1795).

Audiences at theatres and concerts in the 1760s were still predominantly landed or aristocratic in character. However in the last quarter of the century, the upper classes began to desert the public theatre. The diary of Mrs. Katherine Bayly, whose husband was an important official in Dublin Castle, sheds some light on this trend;[32] entries run from the 1720s to 1774. The Baylys were avid theatre-goers and the competition between the two playhouses in the 1760s is duly noted.[33] The family also attended formal venues for music, such as the Great Musick Hall in Fishamble St., the Rotunda, and the Ranelagh Gardens.They frequently attended balls in the Castle and indulged much in card playing.[34] The entries in the diary suggest that theatre attendance by the family began to taper off in the early 1760s.[35]

The account-book belonging to the family of the Hon. Richard Jackson, another Castle official and Derry landowner, is also revealing.[36] The account-book covers the years 1767 to 1778, and shows that the Jackson family, like the Baylys, were socially very active. The period during which they resided in Dublin each year corresponds roughly with the months of the winter season. The Jacksons spent a great deal of money in social activities, and on necessary personal preparations: large sums were spent for instance on hairdressing, and on the hiring of street chairs. The family showed enormous interest in all things musical and were continually hiring dancing and music teachers for their children. They bought season tickets to the Rotunda Balls which cost over five pounds each. They also went to a number of benefit concerts and assemblies. However compared to the Baylys their interest in the theatre was small. They frequently sent their servants to the theatre as a treat, and they recorded the occasional purchase of tickets for plays and operas.

Why the decline in the social tone of public theatre and public performance? Some blamed it on the fact that Lord Lieutenants had, to a large extent, ceased going to the theatre.[37] As with balls and assemblies the expected presence of the Lord Lieutenant at the theatre on a given night was advertised. His

presence acted as a social magnet to the nobility and gentry. By
the mid-1780s, when a theatre evening was advertised as being
'by command of the Lord Lieutenant', it was no longer implied
that the Lord Lieutenant would be present. Between October
and December of 1785 there were five command performances
in the Theatre Royal, Smock Alley, but at this time the Duke
and Duchess of Rutland were touring the country.[38]

The sheer size and relative affluence of Dublin's own
citizens was a major factor in changing both gentry habits and
the season itself. In other words, theatre at least was taken over
by the middle classes. An indication of this is a reference in the
1780s to the fact that 'females of any rank' could obtain a seat
in a box,[39] whereas box-seats had previously been strictly
reserved for 'ladies'.

Many of the gentry turned to amateur dramatics. The Earl of
Westmeath and Frederick Edward Jones founded the Amateur
Dramatics Society in 1792, and opened a subscription list
limited to a hundred gentlemen in order to raise money to
renovate Fishamble St. theatre. The theatre opened in 1794 and
by 1797 it had taken all the box audience away from the public
playhouse.[40] The audience at Fishamble St. was made up
exclusively of nobility and gentlemen. Only the one hundred
subscribers could enter the theatre, accompanied by two female
guests. This worried some, as the convention with public
theatre had been for 'young ladies' to be chaperoned by their
mothers or some older female relative. Now young male
subscribers could bring the daughter or sister of a non-
subscriber without an older relative to check on their
behaviour. Despite some misgivings, amateur dramatics
flourished in the 1790s.

Exclusive entertainments of an informal variety were
probably more lavish and extensive in scale in the 1780s and
1790s than at any other period. The three-year viceroyalty of
the duke of Rutland (1784-87) marked something of a high
point when the extravagant tastes of his wife and himself made
the Castle's social scene more colourful than ever. At the same
time there were a number of aristocratic social centres in the
town, notably Leinster House and Charlemont House, each

with a distinctive style of entertainment. Rutland's Castle saw the introduction of all-night balls as a regular feature, an institution which not all ladies of fashion seem to have approved of. Literally hundreds of guests attended these major 'society' occasions. The French traveller De Latocnaye, on visiting Dublin in 1797, was impressed by the liveliness of upper-class social life, but complained of the indoor conditions:

> where a house might comfortably entertain twenty persons, sixty are invited, and so in proportion. I have seen *routs* [large evening parties] where, from vestibule to garret, the rooms were filled with fine ladies beautifully dressed, but so crushed against each other that it was hardly possible to move...[41]

In April 1785 it was rumoured that the Duke and Duchess of Leinster had given out one thousand double tickets for a masquerade at Leinster House,[42] some indication of the kind of aristocratic entertainment which post-Union Dublin was to remember nostalgicly.

*   *   *

An increasingly popular activity that was mainly associated with winter-time was the fraternal meetings of gentlemen sharing the bond of a common education (Old Etonians were meeting in Dublin in the 1760s),[43] of common regional background (gentry from particular counties often banded together in the capital), or of sporting interest: the 'Sportsman's Club' which met at the Rose Tavern in Dame St. arranged the races and prizes to be run at the Curragh.[44] The Freemasons, who had begun to establish lodges in the capital in the 1720s, included many who had been officers in the army and most Dublin lodges had a distinctly gentry membership. The Friendly Brothers of St. Patrick, an anti-duelling club established in the seventeenth century, had an exclusively gentry membership and met regularly, again at the busy Rose Tavern. All such fraternal associations were tavern-based until the 1780s, but as in the theatre a trend towards a more private, controlled environment then became evident. The gaming club which had begun to meet at Patrick Daly's Tavern in Dame St.

near the Parliament House in the 1760s, soon became the greatest gambling centre in the city, with a membership consisting almost exclusively of M.P.s and their friends. A magnificent new club-house was erected on the site of Daly's between 1789 and 1791, its construction being funded by subscription.[45] The rival 'Kildare St. Club', not to be outdone, planned to build on a similar scale in Westmoreland St.; they remained however in Kildare St. to build sumptuously in the next generation.[46] The withdrawal from the taverns continued into the nineteenth century with lesser clubs also moving into private houses; the Friendly Brothers, for example leased a house in Sackville St. in 1820.[47] The gentleman's clubs usually met for dinner in the late afternoon; this was followed by the endless drinking of toasts which lasted into the early hours of the morning.

*   *   *

The character of the winter season in Dublin was therefore changing in the period under review. 'Aristocratic' venues and activities were no longer dominated by the upper classes towards the end of the eighteenth century, and new, more private, entertainment space was being created. This latter type of social activity was less firmly anchored to Dublin, and after the Union it drifted away from Dublin relatively effortlessly, not least because the life of the wealthy became more peripatetic. One should not exaggerate the importance of the demise of Parliament on these changes in Dublin's season, just as in the era when College Green *was* active, one should not exaggerate the role of Parliament in orchestrating the social season. Dublin's magnetism had always been multifaceted.

NOTES

1.   *Faulkner's Dublin Journal* was carrying the greatest number of advertisements in the 1760s and has been the source used for that decade.

2. See Figure I.
3. *Dublin Evening Post* , 20 May 1784.
4. *D.E.P.*, 15 January 1785.
5. La Tourette Stockwell, *Dublin Theatres and Theatre Customs 1637 -1820* (New York, 1938), p. 182.
6. Ibid., p. 185.
7. *F.D.J.* , January - March 1764.
8. Ibid.
9. T.J. Walsh, *Opera in Dublin 1705 - 87 : The Social Scene* (Dublin, 1973), appendix C.
10. Brian Boydell, 'Music 1700 - 1850', in T.W. Moody and W.E. Vaughan (eds.), *A New History of Ireland, IV: Eighteenth Century Ireland 1691 - 1801* (Oxford, 1986), pp. 596-7.
11. Ibid.
12. Walsh, *Opera,* p.123.
13. Ibid., pp. 210-1.
14. Boydell, 'Music', p. 596.
15. Quoted in Stockwell, *Dublin Theatres* , p. 196.
16. Ibid., p. 209.
17. *F.D.J.* , 15 May 1764. They were well-to-do tradespeople, although in the weeks following the accident there were benefits for the seven children made orphans.
18. Stockwell, *Dublin Theatres* , p. 263.
19. See *D.E.P.* , 13 September 1783 - 1 July 1784.
20. *D.E.P.* , December 1784, various issues.
21. *F.D.J.* , October 1764 - April 1765.
22. *F.D.J.* , May - December 1765.
23. *D.E.P.* , 20 November 1783.
24. Ibid., series of advertisements, February - June 1784.
25. Ibid., 19 February 1785, 4 February 1786.
26. Boydell, 'Music', p. 585.
27. *D.E.P.* , series of advertisements, April - September 1784 and 1785.
28. Ibid., September 1784, September 1785, various issues.
29. Quoted in T. Dawson, 'The City Music and City Bands', *Dublin Historical Record* , XXV (1972), 104.
30. Ibid.
31. I.C. Ross (ed.), *Public Virtue, Public Love : The Early Years of the Dublin Lying-In Hospital* (Dublin, 1986), p. 101.
32. H.F. Berry (ed.), 'Notes from the Diary of a Dublin Lady in the Reign of George II', *J.R.S.A.I.* , 5th ser. VIII (1898), 141.

33.   Ibid., 141.
34.   Ibid., 146.
35.   A list of plays attended by the Bayly family can be found at the end
       of the diary: ibid., 147.
36.   Domestic Account-book of Rt. Hon. Richard and Mrs Jackson,
       1767 - 78 (T.C.D. MS 9218).
37.   Stockwell, *Dublin Theatres* , p. 188.
40.   Ibid., p. 165.
41.   De Latocnaye, *A Frenchman's Walk through Ireland* , ed. John
       Stevenson (Belfast, 1917), p. 20.
42.   J.T. Gilbert, *A History of the City of Dublin* (Dublin, 1859), II,
       305-7; Edward McParland, 'The Wide Streets Commissioners...',
       Qtrly. Bull. Ir. Georgian Soc. XV, 1 (1972), 13 - 14.
44.   Ibid., 18.

The Fashionables, 1795: Scaramouch and Scarecrow (*Walker's Hibernian Magazine,* Sept. 1795).

THE LA TOUCHE DYNASTY

DAVID DICKSON AND
RICHARD ENGLISH

A parliament house too full of gentry, a merchant class too
little regarded by the legislature: such were the complaints of
Dublin merchant and parliamentary candidate James Digges La
Touche in 1748; few or none of his wealthier fellow traders, he
added, 'do bequeath to their children....their business, and
their fame as merchants, for an inheritance.'[1] Conventional as
such observations were, La Touche was no conventional
merchant and his family were unique in the history of Dublin
commerce. His father, David Digges La Touche [hereafter
David I] had settled in Dublin as a Williamite veteran and
became a cloth dealer and wholesale merchant, diversifying in
1716 into banking with three others in the cloth trade, the
leading partner being Nathaniel Kane. This eventually became
the La Touche bank and it remained strictly a family enterprise
for five generations and 154 years, before being absorbed by
the Munster Bank in 1870. The La Touches were perhaps the
wealthiest, certainly the most enduring financial dynasty of
Anglo-Ireland. The breadth of the family involvements in
eighteenth- and early nineteenth-century Ireland was
remarkable, yet despite the singularity of their history, their
fortunes and their fate have wider implications.

James' father, David I, came to Dublin in the 1690s when
the inflow of Huguenot nobles, soldiers and artisans was at its
height. With his noble background, his skills in accounting and
his demonstrable honesty, he came to be the chief Dublin
handler of the pensions and remittances of his fellow refugees.

Out of this developed the formal banking business, which in its early years was not unlike that of other Dublin merchant banks, the discounting and transmitting of bills of exchange and the issuing of bank notes - in other words, moving the monies of long-distance traders and landlords and providing short-term wholesale credit facilities. Profits in the 1720s averaged close to £1,500 per annum for the partnership, on a stock of £8,000.[2]

Most banking partnerships at that period were fairly ephemeral, but the house of Kane and La Touche survived the decades. David I protected his capital by entering the business of property speculation - not in rural land as merchants were so often accused of doing, but in urban leaseholds and freeholds. In the 1720s and 1730s he assembled a largely undeveloped 'land bank' west of St. Stephen's Green, laid it out in streets and building sites, and rented it to building craftsmen, sometimes actually financing them in their construction of large houses for gentry and professional occupation. Other Huguenot speculators were active in the same quarter, but they were dwarfed by the highly profitable operations of the old banker.[3]

David I died in 1745 with a reputation for business rectitude, alms-giving and tenderness towards his debtors that even the Quakers might have envied. Although a member of the French congregation that worshipped in St. Patrick's Cathedral, it was perhaps appropriate that he expired while at prayer in the viceregal chapel, a stone's throw from his Castle Street counting-house.

His two sons, David II and James, who were Dutch educated and had married Huguenot brides, in different ways stepped out of their Huguenot sub-culture. James, despite his father's early hopes that he would follow a literary career, took over the cloth-dealing business and also traded as an import/export merchant from Bachelor's Walk. His father had never taken part in civic affairs (unlike the Kanes), but James was drawn into public life in the 1740s, first as a critic of the municipal governors of the city, then as a parliamentary lobbyist seeking the introduction of Irish bankruptcy laws,

The Private Banks of Castle St., 1788: David La Touche & Co. (left) and
Sir William Gleadowe Newcomen & Co. (right) (*Gentleman's Magazine*,
Dec. 1788).   p.19.

culminating in 1748 with his decision to run as a parliamentary candidate in what became perhaps the most hotly contested by-election in Dublin's history.[4] His running-mate against the aldermanic candidates during the 15-months' long campaign was the radical apothecary Charles Lucas. It was a battle in which both Lucas and La Touche were worsted but a war in which their cause was finally vindicated: in 1760 the government of the city was reformed by Parliament and its constitution made more open.[5] James La Touche's mercantile career faded in the 1750s, but his wealth was revealed after his death in 1763 when an extraordinary art collection came to auction; according to the auctioneer it included among the canvases 2 Van Dycks, 2 Rembrandts, 2 Teniers, a Morillo, a Canaletto and many other Italian and 'Flemish' works.[6] True to his wishes, three of his sons remained in trade, one in Jamaica where he became a plantation owner, one in Dublin as a modest wholesale merchant, and one, William Digges, who made a fortune when based as British representative in Basra (at the head of the Persian Gulf) before returning to Dublin in 1786, where he was accepted into the Castle St. partnership by his banking cousins.[7]

James' elder brother, David II, was closer to his father's mould. He had been left his father's half share in the bank [8] and indeed he remained a banker, keeping outside the parliamentary arena. On or before Nathaniel Kane's death in 1756, he acquired complete control of the bank and later brought in his three sons, David III, John and Peter as equal partners. The reputation of the bank in the city was strengthened by its success in weathering the double bank failure of 1754 and the run on the city banks in 1759/60, an achievement it shared only with the Gleadowe's (later Newcomen's) bank. (Several other financial families resurrected themselves after bankruptcy, but at the cost of tarnished reputations.)

By the early 1770s David II's bank was 'accounted the safest in Ireland',[9] and its status was enhanced by his decision to cater specifically for the needs of landed clientele; he offered not just remittance and discount but also deposit facilities, supplying customers in the later 1770s (if not earlier) blank-cheques for them to draw on the bank at will.[10] As with the modern current account, interest was not paid to clients in credit.[11] Parallelling such London 'West End' banks as Coutts, the La Touche bank seems at the same time to have contracted its mercantile business (although without internal archives for this period, the timing of the transformation is unclear).

With the growing profitability of the bank in the 1750s and 1760s, David II turned away from his father's urban investments and his brother's mercantile priorities, and channelled the profits from the family's bank in the direction from which they were now being increasingly generated: rural land ownership. He purchased property in north Wicklow (where he established a country seat, Bellevue, at Delgany), in north Kildare (Harristown), and in south Leitrim, and the bank became a large-scale mortgagee of rural property, lending to their own clients.[12] By the time of David II's death in 1785, he was said to have a *rental* income of £25,000; by this stage the bank was generating profits of between £20,000 and £30,000 per annum.[13] The elaborate obituaries of Ireland's wealthiest commoner dwelt on his unexampled charity, piety and integrity.[14]

Long before his death, his son David III had taken charge of the banking business. This La Touche entered the Irish Parliament in 1761, buying one of the Dundalk seats for its duration. He purchased seats at three subsequent elections before buying control of the Newcastle (Co. Dublin) borough outright. His financial strength ensured him a place in College Green for forty years until the Union. The motives for his entry into Parliament may have been more specific than his Uncle James' had been: after the hostile 1756 banking act which in effect prevented merchants from describing themselves as bankers or from issuing bank notes, La Touche presumably entered the house to protect the banking interest and build up a financial lobby. Yet married to an non-Huguenot bride and with many parliamentary in-laws, David III became part of Dublin's aristocratic circle, respected for his wealth and his lavish hospitality at his south Dublin retreat, 'Marlay'. His younger brother John sought to enter Parliament the harder

way - by contesting Dublin city in 1767 in a by-election with
the Duke of Leinster's son. John La Touche may well have had
covert Castle support in challenging the 'patriot' Fitzgeralds,
but despite a closely fought campaign, the heir to Leinster
House carried the day.

Through the 1770s the La Touches maintained a coy rather
than a cosy relationship with the government; the Castle view
in 1773 was that David III 'would willingly serve Government
but....has an eye to popularity as it might be of use to his
shop'.[15] An emergency cash loan to the government of
£20,000 in the dark days of 1778 was not augmented when the
Castle sought further credit later in the year. When the Castle
lost control of the Irish Parliament in 1779, David III echoed
the free-trade demands of the opposition majority.[16]

*   *   *

Exchequer crises, constitutional concessions and the other
cathartic consequences of the American war led to the founding
of an Irish version of the Bank of England in 1783. The new
institution was intended to be in effect banker to the
government, manager of the national debt, and a major aid to
commercial liquidity through its issue of bank notes. David III
was involved in the delicate negotiations with the Castle in
1781/2 which had led to the first call for public subscriptions to
the new Bank of Ireland and he was involved in the drafting of
its charter, granted in 1783. With his father, two brothers and a
cousin he led the subscription list : by March 1785 the La
Touches held £48,800 of the total £600,000 of subscribed
stock.[17]

David III was elected the first Governor of the Bank by the
Court of Directors, and his two brothers subsequently became
directors. They retired after two years but he remained as
Governor for eight, despite the preference of some of the
directors for a rotating governorship. La Touche's regime at the
Bank was successful in that the institution grew without crises,
national bank-paper circulation expanded quickly and dividends
rose. But there was no attempt to prevent possible conflicts of

interest between La Touche's private and public concerns - not that he seems to have abused his power beyond nominating his relatives the Pugets (London agents for the La Touches for more than 50 years) as official agents for the Bank of Ireland, while appointing the family's rather mediocre architect, Whitmore Davis, as the overseer of the Bank's buildings. But more insidiously, he may have inspired and certainly supported the discriminatory Bank charter which excluded Quakers and Catholics from the Court of Directors, a decision which split the first directors in 1784.[18] The exclusion of Catholics outlasted David III's regime by over fifty years and was an embarrassing legacy. He left the helm and the Court in 1791, but retained his investment.

David III's politics in the 1780s and 1790s were close to those of the ruling junta in the Castle, particularly to those of Speaker Foster (who as it happened became a large debtor of the La Touche bank in 1793). They shared a belief in the value of the Irish Parliament as an agency for promoting economic development, but were resolutely opposed to a broader definition of the political nation or to any policy that would weaken the status of the Established Church. It was David III who moved the rejection of the Catholic Committee's famous emancipation petition to Parliament in 1792; the naked anti-catholicism of the ensuing Commons' debate marked a turning point in Irish politics and led directly to the Catholic Convention later that year.[19]

Both of David III's brothers eventually joined him in Parliament: John, who had inherited the Kildare estate, purchased the borough of Harristown *circa* 1795 from the man who had defeated him in the Dublin election in 1767, the now financially weakened Duke of Leinster. In the 1797 elections John brought his two sons into Parliament for Harristown and won one of the two Co. Kildare seats for himself at the expense of the Leinster interest.[20] The third brother Peter, who had inherited the Wicklow and Leitrim estates, entered Parliament for Co. Leitrim in 1783, having run as a 'popular' candidate endorsing parliamentary reform;[21] he held the seat with interruptions for the next twenty years. In the last College

Green parliament there were thus five La Touches; all but
David III opposed the Union proposal. Out of doors, their
banking partner and cousin, William Digges, had chaired a
huge meeting of Dublin merchants in December 1798 to
mobilise the city against the Union which, he claimed, 'instead
of strengthening the two countries ... would eventually cause
their separation'. He echoed his cousin David's parliamentary
attack earlier in 1798 on absenteeism; both linked the political
breakdown in the country to the non-residence of the gentry
rather than to more fundamental factors.[22]

Outside the spheres of banking and parliamentary politics
this, the third generation of Irish La Touches had more diverse
social and economic commitments than those before or after. In
1800 William Digges was chairman and David III treasurer of
the Grand Canal Company, and the family were major
investors in the utility.[23] At this time Peter had expanded the
family's interests in Leitrim by purchasing the Arigna
Ironworks from the Court of Chancery *circa* 1793 for £25,000
and laying out, he later claimed, a further £55,000 over the
following fifteen years - with no profit other than Leitrim
freeholders' votes.[24] Within Dublin, the family were founding
members and treasurers of the Kildare St. Club in the 1780s.
In 1800 four members of the family were in the Dublin
Society, three in the Charitable Music Society, four were
governors of the Rotunda Hospital, one (William Digges) a
governor of Dr Steeven's Hospital, one (David) a Wide Street
Commissioner, one (John) the treasurer of the House of
Industry, one (Peter) the treasurer of the Prussia St. Boys'
Orphanage, and one (David) the treasurer of the Lock
Penitentiary (for venereal sufferers).The La Touches had
helped in a major way to finance the Hibernian Marine School
in the 1760s and the Magdalene Asylum (for 'reformed'
prostitutes) in the 1790s; in 1800 there were three family
members associated with the former and two with the latter.[25]
Their role on these bodies was more than as mascots: they gave
hard financial support and their womenfolk much time and
active patronage to the charities they supported. William
Digges, for instance, kept a meticulous record of his small but

diverse charitable donations and subscriptions each year: between 1790 and 1798 his total personal outgoings averaged £4,742 per annum and his 'charity' averaged £155 per annum (or 3.3 per cent).[26] Two members of the next generation became far more heavily involved in moral activity, being early supporters of the evangelical movement: David III's second son John David became a Methodist in 1799, and in the hard winter of 1800/1 he was busily organising assistance for 57 families around Marlay - in the form of coal and bibles.[27] His second cousin James, 'the little Puritan', helped to launch the Sunday School Society in 1808 and was its energetic secretary until his death.[28]

In terms of artistic patronage, the third generation of La Touches hired the best local stuccadores and sculptors for their five town-houses, three around St. Stephen's Green, one in Ely Place and one in Merrion Square, as well as for Marlay, Bellevue, Sans Souci and Harristown. Despite this, and their patronage of the best professional musicians, they were not, all considered, notable leaders of taste.[29] Only Peter, the heir of Bellevue, was swept up by artistic innovation - in the fields of horticulture and landscape design. His massive exotic glass-houses and gardens at Bellevue cost over £4,000 and became a public wonder; however, his most extravagant gesture was to purchase the mountain wilderness around Lough Tay, Co. Wicklow, and to build there a 'gothick' retreat, Luggala, in the early 1790s. He thus helped to bring one dimension of the romantic movement to Ireland.[30]

For the La Touches, as for many families who opposed the Union, the new political arrangements after 1801 actually enhanced their influence. For although they lost their 'pocket' boroughs (in return for £30,000 compensation), their financial strength and the large tenantry on their several estates allowed them to stay in the increasingly expensive business of county politics. They managed to retain three Westminster seats in the post-Union generation, one for Co. Kildare (1801-30), one for Co. Leitrim (1802-20), and one for Co. Carlow (1802-18), giving the family a powerful anti-emancipation voice in the Castle and a say in government patronage.[31] But given their primary role as the Dublin bankers for the nobility and gentry, did not the closure of the Dublin parliament remove some of their clients after 1801?

The fragmentary archives of the bank give a muffled answer. Of the 300 members of the Irish Parliament at its dissolution, 21 per cent of those with names beginning with letters L to Z had held deposit accounts at the La Touche bank in 1789; 19 per cent of those whose names began with letters A to I still held accounts in 1803.[32] We can assume therefore that few accounts were closed in the immediate aftermath of the Union. Of course as major dealers in London-Dublin bills of exchange, the La Touches were well placed to handle the transfer of any rents to England that had previously been spent in Dublin.

Their business was certainly undergoing a major change at this period, for after 1797 the La Touches stopped issuing their own notes and presumably withdrew from bill discounting as well.[33] The Bank of Ireland's decision in 1797 to end the convertibility of notes for gold while the war lasted, precipitated the La Touche withdrawal into a narrower but extremely profitable niche. One indication of the scale of early nineteenth-century operations comes from a day-ledger for 1820/1: between 21 October 1820 and 31 January 1821 £2,427,370 passed through the bank's hands.[34]

Earlier in 1820 many of the private banks that had sprung up during the years of Napoleonic inflation and paper money were forced to close their doors. Even the La Touche partners had feared that the tidal wave of bankruptcy would reach Castle St. They were saved as were three of the four other Dublin private banks by the judicious discretionary support of the Bank of Ireland.[35]

Until the 1820s, apart from the Bank of Ireland, no bank could be owned by more than six partners, but the 1820 collapse and subsequent legislative changes led to the emergence of Irish joint-stock banks - some with branch offices, owned by large numbers of non-participant shareholders. However this process occurred outside the capital because under the terms of the original Bank of Ireland charter no joint-stock competitor, issuing their own notes, could be based in or around Dublin.[36] The La Touches sought to exploit the new situation in the 1820s by accepting the Dublin agency of the London-based Provincial Bank of Ireland. After four years of bitter legal conflict with the Bank of Ireland, they finally won the right to do this. However the ending of the Bank of Ireland's monopoly rights in 1845 and the entry of the new style of banking into the city marked the beginning of a 25-year decline of the Castle St. bank.[37] Just why and how the latter day La Touches failed to rise to the new financial opportunities of early Victorian Dublin remains to be unravelled. The last of the La Touche bankers became socially indistinguishable from the country gentry they had so long served, and they were now to share a common fate.

NOTES

1. [James Digges La Touche], *Two Letters on Trade...* (Dublin, 1748), p.4.
2. David Dickson, 'Huguenots in the Urban Community of Eighteenth-Century Dublin and Cork', in C.E.J. Caldicott, Hugh Gough and J.P. Pitton (eds.), *The Huguenots and Ireland....* (Dublin, 1987), p.326.
3. Ibid., pp.326-7.
4. *Wilson's Dublin Directory, 1753* and *1762;* James Digges La Touche, *Collections of Cases, Memorials, Addresses, and Proceedings in Parliament Relating to Insolvent Debtors...* (London, 1757), pp.49-52; [Charles Lucas], *A Portrait of J[ames] D[igges] L[a] T[ouche]* (Dublin, 1749), p.5.
5. Sean Murphy, 'The Corporation of Dublin 1660-1760', *Dub. Hist. Rec.*, XXXVIII, 1 (1784-85), 26-30.
6. *A Catalogue of the Genuine Collection of Italian, Flemish and Other Pictures of the late James Digges La Touche, Esq. decd. which will be Sold by Auction .....on 16th. May 1764* (Dublin, 1764) [T.C.D. Fag. O. 15].
7. William Urwick, *Biographical Sketches of the late John D. La Touche, Banker* (Dublin, 1868), pp.174-75
8. Public Record Office of Ireland T. 1760, transcript of the will of David Digges La Touche, dated 29 May 1744.

9.   M. Bodkin, 'Notes on the Irish Parliament in 1773', *Proc. R.I.A.,* XLVIII, sect. C (1942), 205.

10.   National Library of Ireland, MS 8544(2).

11.   This statement is based on an inspection of the earliest surviving customer ledgers of 1820-1: Allied Irish Bank Archives, Foster Place, Dublin, Day-book, La Touche's Bank, 1820-1. We are grateful to the board of the Allied Irish Bank for permission to examine the fragmentary La Touche archives, and to Mr. Lambkin, Archivist, for his unfailing courtesy, advice and help.

12.   P.R.O.I. T.1760, transcript of the will of David La Touche [II], dated 2 June 1772.

13.   Ibid., notes on the pedigree of the La Touche family by H.S. Guinness; A.M. Fisher, 'David Digges La Touche, Banker, and a few of his descendants', *Dub. Hist. Rec.,* V, 2 (1943-3), 63.

14.   *Walker's Hibernian Magazine,* July 1795.

15.   Bodkin, 'Irish Parliament', 205.

16.   G.O. Sayles, 'Contemporary Sketches of the Members of the Irish Parliament in 1782', *Proc. R.I.A.,* LVI, sect. C (1954), 208; Edith Johnston,*Great Britain and Ireland 1760-1800....* (Edinburgh, 1963), p.249; R.B. McDowell, *Ireland in the Age of Imperialism and Revolution 1760-1801* (Oxford, 1979), p.268.

17.   *Walker's Hibernian Magazine,* March 1785; F.G. Hall, *The Bank of Ireland 1783-1946* (Dublin, 1949), pp.38, 496-8, 508, 510.

18.   John Ferrar, *A View of Ancient and Modern Dublin....*(Dublin, 1796), p.42; Hall, *Bank of Ireland,* pp.41-3, 118; Edward McParland, 'The Bank and the Visual Arts', in F.S.L. Lyons (ed.), *Bicentenary Essays: the Bank of Ireland 1783-1983* (1983), p.98.

19.   For La Touche's speech, see *Irish Parliamentary Register,* XII, 182. Cf. McDowell, *Ireland,* p.402. For Foster's debt see A.P.W. Malcomson, *John Foster: the Politics of the Anglo-Irish Ascendancy* (Oxford, 1978), p.323n.

20.   G.I. Bolton, *The Passing of the Irish Act of Union* (Oxford, 1966), pp.22, 32.

21.   Edith Johnston, 'Members of the Irish Parliament, 1784-7', *Proc. R.I.A.,* LXXI, sect. C (1971), 189.

22.   *Proceedings of a Meeting of the Bankers and Merchants of Dublin, 18 Dec. 1798* (Dublin, 1798), p.7; Marquis of Londonderry, *Memoirs and Correspondence of Viscount Castlereagh* (London, 1848), II, 47-8; W.E.H. Lecky, *A History of Ireland in the Eighteenth Century* (London, 1892), IV, 226.

23.   *Dublin Directory, 1789* and *1800.*

24. Ferrar, *Dublin*, p.113n.; Issac Weld, *Statistical Survey of County Roscommon* (Dublin, 1832), pp.32-77; McDowell, *Ireland*, p.18.

25. Ferrar, *Dublin*, p.66n.; *Dublin Directory, 1800;* John de Courcy Ireland, 'Maritime Aspects of the Huguenot Immigration into Ireland', in Caldicott et al. *Huguenots*, pp.369-70.

26. N.L.I. MS 19,898, Account-book of William Digges La Touche, 1786-98.

27. N.L.I. MS 3,153, Diary of John David La Touche, Marley, 1799-1801, Loan Fund List 1800/1. John David was later the chief author of the government-commissioned survey of Dublin charities in 1808: John David La Touche et al., *A Report upon Certain Charitable Establishments in the City of Dublin....* (Dublin, 1809).

28. Urwick, *Biographical Sketches*, passim.

29. C.P. Curran, *Dublin Decorative Plasterwork of the Seventeenth and Eighteenth Centuries* (London, 1967), pp.82-4, 86; Brian Boydell, 'Music 1700-1850' in T.W. Moody and W.E. Vaughan (eds.), *A New History of Ireland*, IV: *...1691-1800* (Oxford, 1986), p.585.

30. Ferrar, *Dublin*, pp.98-111; Edward Malins and the Knight of Glin, *Lost Demenses: Irish Landscape Gardening 1660-1845* (London, 1976), pp.168-72.

31. P.J. Jupp, 'Irish M.P.s at Westminster in the Early Nineteenth Century', in J.C. Beckett (ed.), *Historical Studies VII* (1969), pp.66-7.

32. AIB Archives, Index to account holders in La Touche's Bank, 1789 (L-Z only) and 1802 (A-I only).

33. F.W. Fetter (ed.), *The Irish Pound...* (London, 1955), p.15n.

34. AIB Archives, Day-book of La Touche's Bank, 1820-1.

35. Urwick, *Biographical Sketches*, pp.265-7; Charles W. Munn, 'Central Banking in Ireland 1814-50', *Irish Econ. Soc. Hist.*, X (1983), 20-2.

36. Munn, op. cit., 30-2.

37. Hall, *Bank of Ireland*, pp.141-2, 144-8, 252-8.

SACKVILLE MALL:
THE FIRST ONE HUNDRED YEARS

EAMON WALSH

The origins of what is still Dublin's premier street, O'Connell St., formerly Sackville St., are bound up with an eighteenth-century property developer of obscure origins, Luke Gardiner, who accumulated his wealth and vast estates in the first fifty years of the eighteenth century. His banking connections[1] and his lofty position in the Exchequer were the keys to his success in urban land speculation. He developed interests in properties throughout the city - Lazer's Hill, the North Lotts, St. Stephen's Green and Pill Lane among others. His acquisition of a major part of the old St. Mary's Abbey estate 'with all rights and reversions'[2] from the Earl of Drogheda and Lord Duncannon in the 1720s made him the single greatest influence on east-side development in the eighteenth-century city; much of it was prime development land on the edge of the expanding urban core. Gardiner was to prove a very vigorous and imaginative innovator in property development. These qualities were demonstrated in the 1730s when he developed Henrietta St. where twenty-one massive town-houses were built, thirteen by Gardiner himself and eight by his protege, Nathaniel Clements. This new approach by Gardiner, with two terraces of upper-class houses facing one another across a broad street, was to be a major influence on housing fashions and land values.

When the Henrietta St. houses were being erected, Dublin's traffic axis lay due south, along Capel St./Essex

Sackville Mall and Surroundings Streets, 1756 (details from John Rocque's 'Exact Survey of . . . Dublin' (1756)).

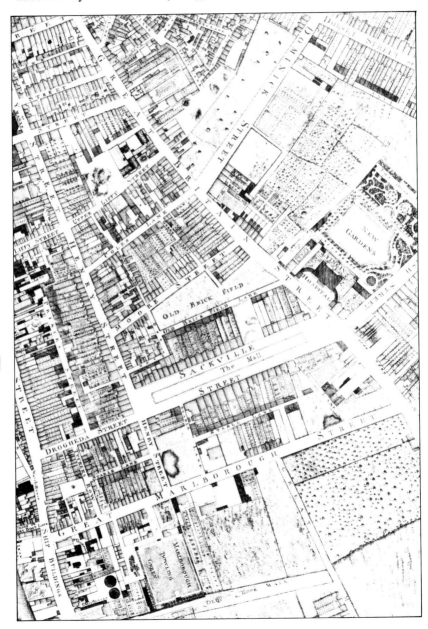

Bridge/Fishamble St., intersected by High St./Castle St. and
Dame St. running eastwards to the Parliament buildings. There
was little development in the north-eastern sector of the city
behind the quays, which in any case were less important than
those on the south side of the river. However the creation of
Marlborough Green marked the beginning of the development
of Marlborough St. and the presence of Lord Drogheda in
nearby Earl St. gave the area some air of exclusiveness.

When Gardiner obtained control of much of the land east of
Capel St. and north of Abbey St., what were his intentions? He
controlled the Drogheda estate for nearly two decades before he
chose to lay out Sackville Mall *circa* 1748-50, the modern
Upper O'Connell St. McParland offers the interesting
proposition that the Mall was a deliberate attempt by Gardiner
to influence a shift of the city centre eastwards;[3] his move
coincided with a parliamentary committee investigating traffic
congestion on and around Essex Bridge.[4] John Bush, writing
in 1769, claimed that Gardiner had intended to extend the street
in its full width to the river.[5] This was of course not carried out
until the 1790s, but there is no explicit evidence of Gardiner's
long-term plans. Dickson has emphasised the speculative
attractions of developing the Mall for its own sake, at a time
when interest rates were unusually low and the demand for
upper-class residential housing was rising sharply:

> Gardiner's declared policy was to lease out building land on very long
> terms, in residential lots, at the highest rents the market would bear,
> avoiding the fining down of rents or the concessionary terms would-be
> improvers often sought.[6]

All we can conclude is that if it was Gardiner's strategy to
influence a shift of the city centre, it was an incomplete one. In
1752 the inhabitants of the Mall had to petition the Corporation
for their own water supply; the Corporation accordingly
'directed that a main be laid down....from Great Britain St.
through the middle of the Mall'.[7] Gardiner died, a wealthy old
man, three years later.

The striking feature of Sackville Mall, as can be seen from
Rocque's Map (Map A), was its width. The emphasis on space
and openness had meant the demolition of many houses not

three-quarters of a century old in what had been the pokey Upper Drogheda St.; much revenue in rents was foregone by laying out such a wide thoroughfare. The new Sackville Mall was one hundred and fifty feet wide, one thousand and fifty feet long, with a pedestrian mall ornamented with lamps and obelisks along the centre. Gardiner encouraged the fashion for wide residential streets that contrasted sharply with the cramped main streets of the older city - Church St., Castle St, or Thomas St. Gardiner's choice of a new name for Drogheda St., Sackville, was a tribute to the English politician Lionel Cranfield Sackville, first Duke of Dorset, who served two terms as Lord Lieutenant, 1731-37 and 1751-55, and in whose administration Gardiner had served. For any planned residential area to be successful in the eighteenth century it needed to be associated with the uppermost echelons of society. Gardiner, a part of the political establishment for thirty years, was very successful in attracting the necessary 'quality' of resident to the Mall. In re-developing the area, Gardiner encouraged the creation of a new civil and Church of Ireland parish, St. Thomas', carved out of the existing St. Mary's. This gave the residents greater control over their parish utilities, policing and taxes. This link between a large-scale property developer and the establishment of a new parish had a Dublin precedent: Joshua Dawson, leading the early eighteenth-century development of land south of Trinity College, had secured the new parish of St. Anne's with boundaries that would protect the interests of wealthy settlers in the parish.

The earliest building initiated by Gardiner on the newly designed Mall was on the east side between Sackville Place and the modern-day Cathal Brugha St. and it was in this area that he took the most interest. (The lower part of this side of the Mall, between North Earl St. and Sackville Place, was not developed in his lifetime; in 1750 it was the back garden and stables of the Earl of Drogheda's house in Earl St., and when this area was developed it contained retail shops from the beginning.) Gardiner was anxious that a substantial part of the street be completed as quickly as possible so as to advertise the Mall. This urgency is reflected in the stipulations of Gardiner's deeds, such as in the lease to Rev. Edward Bayly of 8 May 1750: Bayly undertook that he 'would build for him and his heirs...with all convenient speed from the date, and there erect the walls or shell of a dwelling house...' and that the house would be of brick and stone.[8] Gardiner went so far as to lend money to his lessees in order to speed up construction. In April 1755 he loaned Joshua Cooper £500 to complete his dwelling.[9] By the time of Gardiner's death later that year, this section of the Mall to Cathal Brugha St. was complete.

The east-side development was an impressive sight, all houses being acquired by prominent men of the day who resided in them for at least part of the year. Of sixteen early houses built under Gardiner's eye, no fewer than eight were inhabited by M.P.s in the years following: Joshua Cooper, M.P. for Sligo, was described in 1775 as an 'independent gentleman of considerable fortune - connected in the county interests with Owen Wynne',[10] and indeed, he had Wynne living next door to him. Another M.P. on the Mall was Henry Gore, described in 1775 as a man 'who thinks well of himself but no one else does'.[11] Down the street lived his namesake Frederick Gore, M.P. for Tulsk, one of the mafia of nine Gores, all of whom were members of Parliament in the 1750s.[12] Other notables resident here in the early years were Cromwell Price, M.P. for Downpatrick, Capt. Henry Bellingham, Blaney Townley, M.P. for Carlingford, who succeeded to the wealthy Balfour estates in Fermanagh and Meath in 1789, Hamilton Gorges, M.P., Robert Handcock, M.P. for Athlone (who owned two houses), and banker and alderman Richard Dawson who lived in the mansion at the corner of Sackville Place (see Map A).

There was simultaneous development on the west side of the Mall involving many of the more famous builder-speculators of the day. At the Great Britain St. (Parnell St.) end of the Mall, Nathaniel Clements, Gardiner's partner in the Henrietta St. development, leased a plot on 12 May 1753,

> containing in front to the said Mall 143 feet 4 inches and in the rear to stable land 49 feet 4 inches...boarding to the north Great Britain St., on the south to....Benjamin Burton.[14]

'A Perspective View of Sackville Street and Gardiner's Mall' *circa* 1752 by
Oliver Grace (British Library Coll.).

Clements built two great mansions on the street, later known as
Lifford House and Leitrim House, which became the homes of
Robert Clements, the first Earl of Leitrim and Nathaniel's son.
Other houses further down the Mall were erected in the 1750s
and involved individual builder-speculators such as George
Steward, a carpenter and Alexander Thompson, a plumber.
The Dawson brothers, Richard (killed by a highwayman in
1782) and Thomas, lived on the west side facing their father's
mansion. Nearby their trustee, Sir Lucius O'Brien, M.P. for
Clare, 'a man who disagrees with the rest of mankind by
thinking well of himself'[15] leased ground also on the west side.
He in turn demised a seventy-six foot frontage, plus

> another piece of ground...annexed to the said lease, on which are lately
> built three houses...[in which reside] John Eyre esq., Elizabeth
> Warburton (widow) and Catherine Ormsby (widow)[16]

to Edmund Howard and Hamilton Gorges who seemed to have
subsequently done some speculative building here. The last
house (later divided) at the corner of Henry St. was built by
John Turner who in July 1752 'let unto the said Francis
Morand all that new dwelling house and tenements, situated on
the west side of Sackville St.'.[17] Other prestigious west-side
residents included Benjamin Burton, long M.P. for Carlow and
'one of the most popular and influential men of his day';[18] Dr.
Robert Robinson, at different stages state physician, Professor
of Anatomy at T.C.D., and in 1760 Fellow of the College of
Physicians;[19] members of the powerful Ward family, the noted
political family from Co. Down; and Abraham Creighton,
M.P.

By 1760 the Mall was more than a partial success. Gardiner
had provided the original impetus for a new wave of urban
development that was now being emulated south of the river
with the commencement of a more energetic development of the
Fitzwilliam estate and the laying out of Merrion Square.
Gardiner's two sons continued to be involved in the north-east
city estate which had been divided in two by their father on his
death. Charles oversaw the completion of the north and west of
Rutland Square while Sackville Gardiner worked on Cavendish
Row and the streets to the east. The popularity of the area north

of the Mall was growing and efforts were being made to complete the Mall itself in the early 1760s. A boost to interest in the area was the completion of the New Assembly Rooms beside Dr. Mosse's maternity hospital in 1764.

By the early 1770s Sackville Mall was complete. During the property boom of the mid-1760s, the master-builder George Darley had completed a block of houses on the east side of the Mall (shown as still vacant on Rocque's map). After Luke Gardiner, Darley was the most important influence on the Mall. He leased a number of sites in 1767, and their first inhabitants were Mrs Theresa Gleadowe and Viscountess Netterville, mother of John the sixth viscount, 'supposed to be Roman Catholic'.[20] A later neighbour of the Netterville's, Viscount Southwell, was also it seems, a Catholic.[21] Gervaise Parker Bushe, the young M.P. from Kilkenny and friend of the 'patriot' leader Henry Flood, also occupied a Darley house.

Rocque's Map of 1757 marked a sand-pit owned by John Magill on the west side of the Mall. Between 1769 and 1772 it was leased to Darley and another builder, James Higgens. Four houses were subsequently built here, three of them by Darley. A famous resident of this block was Nathaniel Sneyd, one time M.P. for Cavan, and a partner in the famous wine firm of Sneyd, French & Barton. He inherited the house from his father Edward, and lived here until assasinated by a maniac in Westmoreland St. in 1833.[22] Lodge Evans Morres (later Baron Frankford), M.P. and barrister, lived close by.

The Mall continued to consolidate its position as one of the three or four most prestigious places of aristocratic residence in the city. In 1769 the judicial blow-in from England, Lord Chancellor James Hewitt, Lord Lifford, moved into the Mall around the time he received the freedom of the city in a gold box, 'in testimony of the sense entertained of his distinguished learning, ability, integrity and virtue'.[23] His son and future M.P. Joseph lived with him. His neighbour was Clements' son Lord Leitrim, described in 1775 as 'a peevish, shy retired man'.[24] The Moore family itself re-entered the scene when in 1771 Charles Moore, the sixth Earl of Drogheda, purchased Alderman Dawson's mansion for the very large amount of

£5,000. He was a member of the Hell Fire Club and was described as a rake in his youth.[25] A more inscrutable neighbour was the aging Prime Sergeant, Anthony Malone, 'a man wise and skilful in handling affairs, considers seriously every design'.[26] The Mall also attracted the man who in 1771 became Speaker of the House of Commons, Edward Sexton Pery, described then as having

> a head well filled with Machiavellian brains...is rather bold than bashful, patient, wary and...he is knowing both in the nature of men and in the nature of the state...a shrewd and long-sighted politician.[27]

Not all the Mall's residents were so well thought of by parliamentary contemporaries. Of Thomas Burgh M.P., it was said that

> his manner stands in need of much alteration...as it is highly offensive...arrogant and overbearing...his general knowledge is not very extensive, nor appears to have been labouriously sought after...[28]

Another resident, Sir John Freke M.P., was described as 'for ever drunk and a mere bragger not to be depended on'.[29]

The wealthy, the powerful and the famous continued to come and live on the Mall when in Dublin during the 1770s and 1780s. An index to this popularity can be seen in the number of the Mall's residents who held licences for private sedan chairs in the 1780s. This is one of the best measures of exclusivity at the period. The returns of 1785[30] show that just over 10 per cent of city licence-holders lived on Sackville St. These included the Earls of Belmore, Drogheda (2), Leitrim and Lifford, the Countess of Ross (2), Viscount Sudley, Viscountess Southwell, Sir John Freke, Lady Anne Browne, Lady Tuite, General Massey, E.S. Pery, Edward Ward, Mrs Burton, Mrs Gore, Mrs Madden, Mrs Pearse (decd.), Mrs Pery and Mrs Tilson. In the same year the Dublin Directory recorded ten peers and thirteen M.P.s with addresses in Sackville St. The sedan chair returns for 1787 and 1788 show a similar pattern.[31]

The year 1790 could be the year taken as the high-point of the Mall as an aristocratic residential area. A study of the directories shows that, although the existing aristocratic and landowning residents remained, new residents now came increasingly from the professional and merchant classes.[32] The Directory of 1798 recorded the number of peers at close to the level of 1790 but the number of M.Ps down from 16 to 11. It also shows a rising number of merchants, barristers and doctors giving their address as Sackville St., upper or lower.

The aristocratic tenor of Sackville St. was beginning to change, at first slowly but then by the turn of the century, more obviously. There were several factors behind this but the work of the Wide Street Commission in surveying and re-constructing lower Drogheda St. in the 1780s was the first. The map of 1783 shows Drogheda St. as a narrow congested street barely reaching the river. But the Directory Map of 1785 shows the improvements made in widening the street to match the Mall. In 1795 Carlisle Bridge was opened and this now connected Sackville St. with the Houses of Parliament. Thus John Ferrar wrote ecstatically in 1796 that

> the grand improvement was made in the year 1795, in Sackville St..., the boast of the city...The continuation of this street to Carlisle Bridge and from thence to Stephen's Green, is a work of utmost utility, uniting the eastern parts of the town, which were divided by the river.[33]

This ripped open Gardiner's closed residential Mall and quickly made it a popular and busy thoroughfare. New Sackville St. (Lower Sackville St.) was from the beginning much more commercial in its character. The Mall itself had had a history of some non-residential activity: the Directory of 1770 listed Evans & Dornans as sugar bakers trading on the Mall (but they had gone by 1773; whether their sugar-house was there remains doubtful). In 1772 Catherine Bourke,[34] grocer, is recorded in the Directory on the Mall, and in 1780 her business was, it seems, taken over by H. Clements.[35] With the widening of the street to the river, the Mall became a popular place for visitors and this acted as a stimulus to commerce. This is especially true of Lower Sackville St. which became almost exclusively a shopping precinct.

The popularity of the Mall as a place of public resort developed markedly with the bridge's construction. The changed tone of the street was described in the *Dublin Satirist* of November 1809:

> Here the rich and poor, the gay and giddy of each sex resort, here they
> take the dust by way of taking the air...If a Munster or Connaught
> beauty arrives who is ambitious of admiration, where can she expose
> her charms with such effect as on the Mall?[36]

In so far as the well-to-do sought tranquillity, the Mall's
attractions were declining. However, the street was ideally
placed for the new kind of larger shops. The aristocracy were
being attracted to newer and quieter areas to live, notably by the
managers of the Fitzwilliam estate and by Luke Gardiner II,
grandson of the first Luke who, before his death in 1798, was
supervising the building of Mountjoy Square, Gardiner St, and
terraces adjoining. In such newer developments building leases
not only set out construction specifications, but prohibited
industry or businesses that might despoil or cheapen the
environment. Flood has pointed out that health and clean
surroundings were now influencing the choice of residency
much more strongly than in the previous generation.[37] The
premium on good sanitation increased during the early
nineteenth century, and Sackville Mall had many limitations:

> for want of sewers, the filth and water were received in pits, called
> cesspools, dug before the doors and covered in and those continued in
> Sackville St...long after 1810, and many now remember the horrid
> sight and smell which periodically offended the inhabitants...when
> those stygian pools were opened and emptied.[38]

The residents of Sackville Mall who wished to leave could sell
their property or sub-let it quite easily, as the Mall remained in
the highest bracket of rateable value in the first half of the
nineteenth century. An examination of Griffith's Valuation of
1854 shows that nearly all those listed as occupiers then were
sub-letting from others; practically none of those listed as
immediate lessors actually lived on the street.[39] The ownership
of many houses remained in the families of the original lessees.
For instance, number 11 remained in Owen Wynne's family
for nearly eighty years.

The old lifestyle of upper-class residents in Sackville Mall
had been expensive. A pamphlet on the proposed Act of
Union, written in 1799, attempted to assess the spending
power that would be lost to Dublin on the passing of the act,

TABLE I

Estimate of House Values and Annual Expenditure of Peers and M.P.s Resident in Sackville Street, 1795-99

Name	'Annual Expenditure that will be lost'	'Value of Property to be sold & taken elsewhere'
PEERS		
Marquis of Drogheda	£3,000	£5,000
Earl of Glandore	£2,500	£2,500
Earl of Leitrim	£4,000	£4,000
Earl of Belmore	£4,000	£3,000
Viscount Gosford	£2,000	£2,000
Viscount Pery	£2,500	£3,000
Baron Sunderlin	£2,500	£3,000
COMMONS		
Alexander Hamilton	£1,000	£2,000
Archibald Acheson	£1,000	£2,000
William Burton	£1,500	£3,000
Blayney Balfour	£1,500	£3,000
J.O. Vandeleur	£1,500	£2,000
Robert Alexander	£2,500	£3,000
Lodge Evans Morres	£1,500	£3,000
Gilbert King	£1,000	£1,000
Henry Coddington	£1,000	£1,000
Denis Browne	£2,000	£2,000
Arthur Dawson	£2,000	£3,000
Owen Wynne	£1,000	£1,000
Thomas Burgh	£1,500	£3,000
J.S. Rochford	£1,000	£1,500
Issac Corry	£3,000	£3,000
TOTAL	£43,500	£56,000

Source: 'Dublin will lose by the Union', P.R.O.N.I. D207/10/9.

Note: No information was given on the following who were or who had normally been resident on the street: Viscount Southwell; Viscount Netterville; Nathaniel Sneyd, M.P.; General Eyre Massey, M.P.; John Dunn, M.P.; Thomas Knox, M.P.; and Cromwell Price, M.P.

and residents and ex-residents of the Mall were prominent on the list.[40] (see Table I).

The first major transformation in the 'quality' of the street's residents is notable in the Directory of 1798 and it concerns those involved in the legal and medical professions. Four barristers, nine solicitors and eight other members of the legal profession were new residents in the street; the opening of the Four Courts on its present site in 1796 saw a gradual move by the legal profession from the south to the north side of the river. The commercial and business premises were also on the increase; thus one finds Anne Gorden, 'milliner and mantua maker', advertising in *Saunder's Newsletter* on 26 January 1798, that her premises were next door to the Marquis of Drogheda.

The Act of Union was also something of a spur to the exodus of aristocracy from Sackville St. The Directory of 1800 listed six peers, eight M.P.s, four members of the Corporation, six members of the medical profession, twelve in the legal profession and twenty-three business persons as resident on the street. Members of the aristocracy may have maintained houses on the street, but the amount of time they actually lived in them was presumably declining. The Directory of 1805 lists four M.P.s as giving their Dublin address as Sackville St., but it is doubtful whether Archibald Acheson, Nathaniel Sneyd, Denis Browne or John Foster spent enough time in these houses to be called residents. The same can be said of the five peers, the Marquis of Drogheda, the Marquis of Sligo, the Earl of Leitrim, Baron Sunderlin and Viscount Pery, who gave Sackville St. as a Dublin address. Such people were spending more time in London or on their country estates in Ireland. When in Dublin, the aristocracy were moving to quieter areas of the city, such as Lodge Evans Morres, Baron Frankford, now resident in Merrion Square, and Viscount Corry who was now in Rutland Square. The people who spent their lives on the street were now doctors, barristers and solicitors. Robert Alexander, the very wealthy wine merchant and director of the Bank of Ireland; John Cash, a former city sherriff; John Bagot, breeches-maker; and Robert Norris, hatter, are more representative of the street's residents. The 1805 Directory records some thirty to forty businesses being carried on in the street, with three hotels and an insurance office as well. By 1810 practically no politician or peer of note resided on the street; the Marquis of Sligo had gone, dividing his time between Grafton St., London and Westport House in Co. Mayo; the Earl of Leitrim's Dublin abode was now at Leixlip.

Sackville St. had changed from a prestigious residential area to a prestigious commercial area. In a sense it followed the fortunes of the city as it became a less aristocratic and more professional place. On Sunday evenings music was provided in the street by military bands[41] and the fame of the street's shops was beginning to attract comment. Thus wrote William Gregory in 1815:

> the shops are handsomely fitted up with considerable taste, and so near are the resemblance of several streets to some [in London]....that a stranger from that city might imagine he was in London.[42]

This image was actively cultivated. The Poor Enquiry of 1836 reported that Sackville St. shop-owners employed inspectors to keep the street clear of beggars.[43] But not everyone was happy with the diversification of function that was taking place on the once premier residential Mall. Wright, commenting in 1821, claimed that

> the city was thrown into great confusion and disorder, by the introduction of the act of Union...The measure has changed the appearance of Dublin; with the removal of its Parliament, the nobility of Ireland withdrew to England, and left their places in Dublin either to fall to decay or be converted into public offices, hotels or charitable institutions.[44]

He listed four hotels in upper Sackville St. alone - those of Thomas Gresham, Christopher Bilton, Matthew Crosbie, and George Jones' 'Waterford Hotel'. Another of the disgruntled was resident Michael Malley, who gave evidence to the 1823 Parliamentary Committee on Local Taxation;[45] he complained that the people on the Mall were being rated far too heavily. He said he paid more tax than Lord Norbury in Denmark St. or Baron McClelland in Gardiner Place; tax, he pleaded, 'falls much less heavily on the more wealthy part of the inhabitants

than it does on the poor'.[46] But such sweeping statements can
be dangerous; with reference to the street in 1815, it was
recorded how 'it was supposed by many that one of the effects
of the Union, would be a reduction of rents and fines, yet both
have been very much raised'.[47]

As the century progressed the number of purely residential
buildings on the Mall fell. By 1830 there remained little more
than a dozen houses that were primarily residential in the Mall
part of the street. To appreciate the degree of diversification it is
interesting to see how some of the great houses of the Mall
changed over the period (see also Appendix I). Drogheda
House was divided into two (numbers 9 & 10) after the Earl's
death in 1822. In 1844 one part was occupied by W. Curry,
the publisher and bookseller, the other part by the Hibernian
Bible Society. The next house was the Hotel & Livery Stables
of Mrs Kezia Reynolds. Beyond that in number 15 was the
clubhouse of the Friendly Brothers, (now in St. Stephen's
Green). Number 16 had been the Dublin Institution since 1811,
a literary and scientific library where, 'the most unrestrained
freedom of conversation was allowed...and discussions were
carried on with less moderation than some members...thought
comported with the privacy and silence of a literary
institution'.[48] By 1844 this and the house next door formed the
Committee Houses for Charitable Societies. In 1830 number
19 had become the Waterford Hotel and Royal Mail Coach
Office. The other hotel on the east side of the Mall was the
Gresham Hotel. Thomas Gresham, who had been abandoned
as a baby on the steps of London's Royal Exchange, purchased
two houses and united them as one in 1817. Later he leased
another one next to these, which was used as a place of
seclusion for visiting gentry.[49]

On the west side of the street, we find that by 1850 Lifford
House has been divided, one building being vacant, the other
occupied by John Smith, wine merchant and grocer. Leitrim
House became a hotel in 1820 after being occupied by the
Commissioners for the Issue of Money. Alderman Burton's
mansion had become the offices of the Richmond Institute for
the Industrious Blind and of the Royal Agricultural

Improvement Society. In 1844 number 53 was the Commercial Mart Co. and next to this the Dorset Institute. Robert Heinkey's Bilton Hotel was in number 56, next to Thwaite's Mineral Water factory. Richard Dawson's house was in 1850 the Sackville Club, (there had in fact been a clubhouse here since the late 1790s). The last great institute on the Mall was the Cow-Pock Institute which

> opened the 14th of February 1804, for the gratuitous inoculation of the poor and for supplying the different parts of the kingdom with genuine infection.[50]

Between 1830 and 1850, the street was progressively abandoned as a residential area by the wealthier merchants, barristers and professionals. They kept their offices and businesses on the street, but increasingly lived elsewhere. This trend was helped by the opening in 1834 of the Dublin & Kingstown Railway. People were now commuting much longer distances to their places of employment and business. In 1849 James Kirby had a rocking-horse factory on the Mall, but lived at Tritonville, Sandymount; in 1851 John Meaz, bootmaker, had his shop in number 2 and his home in 10 Tivoli Terrace East, Kingstown; Thomas McNury of number 11, merchant, lived in Rathmines.

There was a change not only in the social mix of the people in Sackville St. but a religious and political one also. We have two snap-shots of the political composition of the Mall, far apart in time. In the 1760s when the street was overwhelmingly Church of Ireland and landed, votes in the parliamentary elections went to 'establishment' candidates - to the city recorder and Burton rather than to Dunn or Lucas in 1761;[51] in the 1767 by-election voting was divided fairly evenly between the duke of Leinster's son and John La Touche.[52] But the vastly different circumstances of 1835[53] give a much better insight into religious and political demography. Votes for the pro-Repeal ticket of Daniel O'Connell and Edward Southwell Ruthven on the Mall were slightly out-numbered by the anti-Repeal support for G.A. Hamilton and J.B. West. From this we can assume then that a majority of those who lived on Sackville St. were Protestant and Tory, although wealthy

Catholic middle-class families were also present such as Valentine O'Connor's.

In 1850 Sackville St. was the 'romantic' centre of Dublin, with the Pillar and the great doric General Post Office symbolising the centre of Dublin. It was still the premier commercial and business street and host to many and varied activities. Some complained about the loss of the aristocratic tone of the Mall, but it could still stir the admiration of contemporaries such as Whittock who in 1846 classed it as 'the grandest street in Dublin, from its width and size, and elegance of the houses on each side'.[54]

NOTES

1. Gardiner's banking partner was Arthur Hill. The bank went into voluntary liquidation in 1737.
2. Nuala Burke, 'Dublin 1600-1800: A Study in Urban Morphogenesis', (unpublished Ph.D. thesis, University of Dublin 1972), p.220.
3. Edward McParland, 'Strategy in the Planning of Dublin, 1750-1800', in Paul Butel and L.M. Cullen (eds), *Cities and Merchants*....(Dublin, 1986), p.98.
4. The report of this committee was the first attempt to influence a major eastward shift of the city.
5. McParland, 'Strategy', p.78.
6. David Dickson, 'Large-Scale Developers and the Growth of Eighteenth-Century Irish Cities', in Butel and Cullen, *Cities*, p.116.
7. J.T.Gilbert (ed), *Calendar of the Ancient Records of Dublin*, X, 19.
8. Registry of Deeds, Dublin, 141/141/94728.
9. Rg. Deeds, 172/362/116812.
10. William Hunt (ed), *The Irish Parliament in 1775* (Dublin, 1907),p.14.
11. Mathew Bodkin (ed), 'Notes on the Irish Parliament in 1773', *Proc. R.I.A.*, XLVIII, sect. c. (1942-3), 204.
12. Georgian Society, *Records of Eighteenth-Century Domestic Architecture and Decoration in Dublin* (Dublin, 1909-13), III, 85.
13. Ibid., 83.

14. Rg. Deeds, 160/294/107351.
15. Bodkin, 'Notes', 204.
16. Rg. Deeds, 208/147/137738.
17. Ibid., 156/164/104036.
18. Georgian Society, *Records*, III, 88.
19. *Dublin Directory for 1760.*
20. G.O. Sayles (ed), 'Sketches of Members of the Irish Parliament in 1782', *Proc. R.I.A.*, LVI, sect. c. (1954), 280.
21. Ibid., 282.
22. Georgian Society, *Records*, III, 92.
23. Gilbert, *Ancient Records*, XIII, 22.
24. Hunt, *Parliament*, p.13.
25. Georgian Society, *Records*, III,
26. Bodkin, 'Notes', 218.
27. Ibid., 202.
28. [Rev. John Scott], *Review of the Principal Characters in the Irish House of Commons* (Dublin, 1789), p.85.
29. Bodkin, 'Notes', 181.
30. *An Account of the Subsisting Licenses for Private Sedan Chairs, 25 March 1787* (Dublin, 1785).
31. *Account of Sedan Chairs, 15 March 1787* (Dublin, 1787); *Account....1788* (Dublin, 1788).
32. For example in 1795 the new residents of the Mall can be clearly discerned: they consisted of 3 barristers, 6 soliciters, 1 wine merchant and 1 dentist.
33. John Ferrar, *View of Ancient and Modern Dublin* (Dublin, 1796), p.36; for the background to the 1785 decision of the Wide Streets Commissioners to extend the Mall to the river, and for details of the architectural planning of what became Sackville St. Lower, see Edward McParland, *James Gandon: Vitruvius Hibernicus* (London, 1985), pp.87-93.
34. The *Directory* for 1777 gives the address as no. 1. We presume her to be on the west side of the Mall at Nth. Earl Street, though the system of numbering before 1800 was inconsistant and underwent changes.
35. Listed in the *Directory* for 1780 as H. Clements, grocer, 1 Sackville St.
36. Quoted in Constantia Maxwell, *Dublin under the Georges* (3rd. ed. London, 1946), p.116.
37. D.T. Flood, 'The Decay of Georgian Dublin', *Dub. Hist. Rec.*, XXVI-VII, (1972-4), p.91.

38. G.N. Wright, *An Historical Guide to Ancient and Modern Dublin* (London, 1821), p.8.
39. *Primary Valuation, Dublin City* (Dublin, 1854), pp.84 et seq.,125-7.
40. P.R.O.N.I. Foster Papers, D207/10/9: 'Dublin will lose by the Union'.
41. Maxwell, *Dublin*, p.116.
42. W. Gregory, *Picture of Dublin* (Dublin, 1815), p.50.
43. Jenny Price, 'Dublin 1750-1850: Spatial Distribution and Organisation of Economic Activity', (unpublished M.Sc., University of Dublin 1980), p.82.
44. Wright, *Guide*, p.8.
45. *First Report of Select Committee on Local Taxation in the City of Dublin* (Brit. Parl. Papers 1823, VI), pp.136-44.
46. Ibid., p.139.
47. Gregory, *Picture*, p.65.
48. J. Warburton, J. Whitelaw and R. Walsh, *History of the City of Dublin* (London, 1818), II, 943.
49. An example of an hotel bill of that period is that of a Major Semple who in July 1834 spent three nights with dinner including sherry and Madeira wine for which he was charged £1.14s.11/2d: *Evening Press*, 11 June 1980.
50. *Pigot's Directory, 1824*, p.120.
51. *Alphabetical list of the Freemen and Freeholders of....Dublin polling 22 April to 6 May 1761* (Dublin, 1761), [N.L.I.].
52. *Alphabetical list of the Freemen and Freeholders who polled in the City Election of 1767* (Dublin, 1767), [N.L.I.].
53. *List of Voters for the Election for the City of Dublin* 12-17 January, 1835 (Dublin, 1835).
54. Price, 'Dublin', p.85.

APPENDIX I

Notes on the Evolution of 5 Houses in Sackville Mall, 1751 - 1854

DATE   OCCUPIER/BUSINESS   STATUS

House Nos. 9/10 (Drogheda House): east side corner of Sackville Place

1751-1756	Ald. Richard Dawson	Residential
1771-1822	Charles, 6th. Earl of Drogheda	ditto
1824-1830	Mrs. Wilson	ditto
1830-1832	James Barton esq.	ditto
1832-1833	Mrs. Cox	ditto
1833- on	[no. 10] Hibernian Bible Society	Office
1833-1843	[no. 9] William Curry	Booksellers & Publishers
1844-1846	[no. 9] J. McGlashen	ditto
1849-1850	[no. 9] G. Herbert	Inks Agent
1852- on	[no. 9] J. Torry	Coal Agent

House No. 35 (built 1767): east side, nr. Cavendish Row

1785- on	A. O'Donnell esq.	Physician
1818-1820	R. Butler & Sons	Medical Hall
1820-1826	J. & C. Butler	ditto
1826-1832	W. Williams	Silk Mercer
1831-1834	Trenor & Wanne	Milliners & Dressmakers
1835- on	Mrs. S. Trenor	ditto
1837-1841	Mrs. Mathews	Milliner
1839-1840	F. Roper & Co.	Merchant Tailors
1840- on	W. Cornish	Stationer
1841- on	W. Hayes	Law Stationer
1842-1846	G. de Barr	ditto
1842-1845	Anne Wall	Milliner
1847- on	F. Bowen	Cigar Importer
1848- on	W. Gibbons	ditto
1849- on	Webb & Co.	Boot & Shoemakers

DATE	OCCUPIER/BUSINESS	STATUS

House No. 46 (built 1769); west side, on site of 'sand pit'

1769- on	Lodge E. Morres, Baron Frankfort	Residential
1798- on	Mervyn Pratt esq.	ditto
1823-1834	Sneyd, French & Barton	Wine Merchants
1835- on	French, Barton & Co.	ditto

House No. 51: at middle of west side

1752-1754	John Turnace	Builder
1754-1763	Abraham Creighton, M.P.	Residential
1763- on	Nicholas Price esq.	ditto
1794-1835	J. Lindsey esq.	ditto
1836- on	H. & V. O'Connor	Merchants
1839-1844	Mrs. H. O'Connor	(?)

House No. 53: west side, south of No. 51

1752- on	Gustavus Brooke esq.	Wine Merchant
1785-1799	A. L. Corry, Earl of Belmore	Residential
1799-1816	J. Connolly	Merchant
1816-1826	Mr. O'Connor	(?)
1826- on	Commercial Mart Co.	Office
1832-1834	'Commercial Building'	Hotel & Tavern
1834- on	F. H. Emerson	Stationer
1835-1839	J. J. Butler Marshall of Dublin	Stores
1837-1841	J. Ward	Surgeon & Dentist
1842-1843	W. Pullen	Tavern
1844-1845	Albert Hotel	Hotel
1846- on	Hibernian Railway Co.	Office
1847- on	G. W. Hemains, Civil Engineer	Office
1848-1849	G. W. Willoughby, Civil Engineer	Ditto

Sources: Registry of Deeds, Deed Books 1750-75; St. Thomas' Grand Jury Cess Books, 1823-34 (P.R.O.I. M.4940-55); Chart Transcripts of 1851 Enumerators' Returns, Dublin (P.R.O.I. CEN/1851/18/1); *Directories* at large, 1753-1853; *Griffith's Valuation*, 1854; Georgian Society, *Records*, III (1911).

WOMEN IN THE WORKFORCE

IMELDA BROPHY

It is the conventional wisdom that in nearly every European city before the factory age the labour force had one standard feature: widows and unmarried women were to be found in a vast variety of unrewarding occupations, and that these women, who were forced to become wage earners, received decidedly smaller rewards for equivalent labour than men did. The assumption seems to have been that women's work was devalued because, to quote a writer on London women, 'they had no experience of combinations, no sacrosanct customs, no tradition of formal apprenticeship - all of which establish a skill'.[1] The skilful tasks, even in the finer branches of the clothing trades, could not command a premium wage because of the marginalised position of working women and the very limited industrial leverage they possessed.

To what extent does eighteenth- and early nineteenth-century Dublin fit this picture? Leaving aside upper-class women of leisure and their personal servants, how far were the women of the city involved in the formal economy, and to what degree were they the powerless cogs of a male world of business?

To discover the extent of women's involvement in wholesale and craft trades in the city between 1750 and 1850, data on a group of 50 women were examined. The women in question are those who were listed in the *Dublin Directory* of 1800. Previous mentions in the directories were traced to determine their first entry into business and subsequent mentions to find when their involvement ceased, the main purpose being to establish how they came to be in a position of ownership and to what extent they operated independently of male relatives.

The trades they were associated with turned out to be mainly in the general area of clothing and textiles, as it was only here that women could compete with men and in some cases establish a numerical pre-eminence; there was however, a minority involved in other, more traditionally 'male' trades. The trade directories do not allow for a comprehensive study of the situation as some trades were slow to change their directory entries and not all traders chose to advertise their business in the directories. However, the lack of other material on the subject necessitates a heavy reliance on this source. The trade directories, published yearly from the mid-1750s, contain the names and addresses of several thousand merchants and traders in the city and the nature of their business - these were mainly, but by no means exclusively male.

The following figures emerged from the 1800 group. Of the 50 female-led businesses, 27 had never it seems been listed as owned by a man or men, 22 businesses had previous male ownership, and 1 had previous female ownership. After 1800, 37 remained in the same hands before completely disappearing from the directory, 8 were subsequently taken over by men, and 5 were continued by other women.

The fact that several women in this sample took over a business on the death of the husband or father points to their regular involvement in it during his lifetime. Unlike the Victorian period and after - when female participation in commerce was frowned upon - the involvement of women in trade would seem to have been fairly widely accepted. In pre-industrial society businesses were smaller family-centred activities and economic necessity forced a widow to continue her husband's business where possible - in an age which was only beginning to develop life assurance schemes and other forms of family financial protection.

Widows often informed customers of their continuation in business through newspaper advertisments. In 1767

Catherine Black, widow of James Black, late Deputy City Appraiser and Auctioneer, has succeeded her husband in said employment with the assistance of her brother. Any person trying to appraise goods will be prosecuted according to law...none other having lawful power to appraise. Anyone wanting to auction goods should call on her brother. She still furnishes funerals.[2]

Obviously Mrs. Black had the necessary expertise to continue in business on the death of her husband and could combine apparently disparate skills. Advertisements of this kind were to be found in the newspapers throughout the period, women often employing a male relative to run the more public side of the business. In some cases a woman succeeding to a business switched it to a more traditionally female-dominated area, usually some branch of the clothing trade. This trend is typified by the case of Ann Bingham who took over her husband's iron-mongery business on his death in 1800. The trade directories for the following five years give her trade as linen draper, that of iron monger being only re-introduced in 1805 when her son came into partnership with her. The drapery business continued to function after 1805 with Ann Bingham apparently retaining ownership.[3]

Marriage was usually a business contract and people tended to marry others with similar occupations, thereby ensuring that the skills of both partners would complement each other. This is especially true during the early decades of the period when most artisanal activity was carried out in the home and involved both husband and wife. Thus a number of women, more usually widows, were to be found in such occupations as butchers, plumbers, furriers, skinners, goldsmiths - trades that gradually became more male-dominated. But as the family wage increasingly became that of the male breadwinner the woman's position within the family power structure was reduced. This is reflected in amendments to the succession laws which over the period made it increasingly difficult for women to inherit and bequeath property. An act passed in the Irish Parliament in 1695 declared void the Irish 'custom' of a wife's right to inherit one half of her husband's property and two-thirds if there were children. A further act of 1833 made it more difficult for property to be inherited through the female line and in 1837 it became unlawful for a married woman to make a will.[4]

Ownership of large-scale business concerns by women was somewhat more common in the eighteenth than in the nineteenth century. Involvement in the family trade since childhood seems to have been normal, in some instances perhaps enhancing a woman's chance of inheritance. In the case of Mary Knabbs, a Dublin linen printer whose mother, having 'carried on a great linen and printing business at Palmerstown', died suddenly in 1753, a dispute arose as to who should inherit the business. Basing her claim on the fact that she and her mother had managed the linen works together prior to her mother's death, Mary Knabbs proved her right to inherit. Interestingly enough, one of her brothers, also the owner of a linen printing works, died intestate and the administration of his estate was taken over by his daughter in 1776.[5]

There is also the case of Catherine Bond, a thread manufacturer whose husband petitioned the Dublin Society on her behalf in 1763 for a financial subvention as she was unable to travel. He seems to have had no involvement in her business. He stated in the petition that she had been involved with yarn-making 'since her infancy', and that 'she is assisted by her four daughters so that she can carry on the whole manufacture before her own eyes'.[6]

A further example of female enterprise is that of Margaret Ashworth who took over her husband's linen-printing works on his death in 1764, and successfully ran the business until 1793.[7] In these and other instances from the eighteenth century onwards, women were apparently unrestricted in their access to training and ownership of their businesses, and were as likely to have learned the trade from their parents as to have acquired it through marriage.

Of the various branches of skilled employment where women could operate independently of men, the clothing trades were by far the most important. The 1841 census records 32.2 per cent of the female workforce in Dublin City employed in this area compared to 17.8 per cent of the occupied male

The Informal Sector: Women Street Vendors, *circa* 1775 (*J.R.S.A.I.*, 5th. ser. (1925),).

workers. 'Clothing trades' included seamstresses, dressmakers, milliners, lace makers, tassel makers, staymakers and bonnet makers (see Appendix I). In terms of the amount of money involved, the millinery trade was the most important and it was here that women established in effect a monopoly. There were 130 female-owned millinery shops in the city in 1841, directly employing some 700 women. In London in 1761, the fee to apprentice to a milliner was put at between £40 and £50, and the capital required to set up in business afterwards estimated to be from £100 to £1,000. Many women trained in this area but remained journeywomen for life.[8] This was also true of other trades and the same trend existed in Dublin. The prospects of those who remained journeywomen were extremely poor. One writer in 1747 cautioned parents in London not to put their daughters into the haberdashery business unless they could set them up as shopowners afterwards, for as in the millinery trade, despite the large profits they themselves made, owners paid those under them extremely badly:

> although a young woman can work neatly at all manner of needlework yet she cannot earn more than 5s. to 6s. a week out of which she is to find herself in board and lodging.[9]

These women employed at 'all manner of needlework' extended from the poorest roomkeepers to the wives and daughters of artisans. Much of this work, especially during the busy social season, was carried out at home and, except in the case of artisans' wives, was for the women involved their only means of income.

In other trades where sewing was part of the process, women and girls were employed in large numbers in what were the more tedious and wretchedly paid tasks. In the glove trade for example men's work was connected with tanning, staining and cutting the leather while women were employed at sewing. In London the Charter of Incorporation granted to glovers in 1638 expressed disapproval of the practice of female apprenticeship so that by the eighteenth century few women attained the position of master glover by apprenticeship.[10] This was also true for Dublin and by 1841, according to the census, only one female glover traded in the city compared with 22 men, whereas there were 248 female operatives and only 44 males employed in the trade.[11] Data on wage differentials are very difficult to interpret, as we do not know whether men and women performed identical tasks; there is no doubt however that women's wages in these trades were substantially lower than men's: in 1800, male glovers in Dublin received a wage of £1.12s.6d. per week, female glovers 14s., i.e. about two-fifths of the former; in the depressed and deflationary 1830s the wages were 12s. and 6s. respectively, a narrowing if anything, of the differential.[12] The same was true for other trades such as coach-making, where men did the skilled carpentry work and were being paid accordingly, women did the 'unskilled' sewing of the upholstery. In staymaking, which was skilled work mostly done by men, women did much of the sewing. It was considered that 'the work is too hard for women, it requires more strength than they are capable of, to raise walls of defense about a lady's shape, which is liable to be spoiled by so many accidents'.[13] As in London this changed in the nineteenth century and the trade became almost completely dominated by women, the main reason being that lighter stays came into fashion. By 1841 there were 43 female and 4 male staymakers in Dublin, whereas in 1760 there had been no women staymakers and 24 men (see Table I).

The growth of trade combinations in Dublin among skilled male artisans in the mid- and late eighteenth century threatened women's access to workshop employment. Journeymen came to view their interests within a trade as distinct from those of the masters as the prospects of all eventually becoming masters faded and as the regulatory role of the guilds over masters who flouted the apprenticeship conventions disappeared. The threat posed to skilled artisans by the growth of an unskilled labour force in the city caused many journeymen combinations to agitate against the employment of women and of outsiders in the same breath. Giving evidence to the Commons' Grand Committee of Trade in 1782 when it was investigating the activities of Irish combinations, one Dublin worsted manufacturer pointed out that combinations in that trade in the

1760s and after had caused all the city women to lose their jobs for no reason other than the fact that male journeymen felt 'the women had not a right to work at men's work, it was their inheritance'. The fact that the manufacturer in question felt that 'the women did most parts of the weaving better than the men, more diligently and cleaner'[14,] may have been a reason for the male employees' discontent. Did the well-entrenched male weavers see women workers, lacking the experience of assertive collective action, as too inclined to accept lower wages and poorer conditions? In 1820 journeymen tailors demanded from their employers a prohibition on the introduction of women or of 'unqualified' men into the trade.[15] One master tailor noted in 1836 that 'the regulations among the journeymen tailors prevent the employment of women in any branch of that trade. There have been many times when the men would strike in any shop which gave employment to women'.[16] The evidence of a shipbuilder in the same year echoed this:

> About fifteen years ago I had a woman in my employ who had been threatened in consequence of working at the trade - I found it necessary to escort her to her lodgings.[17]

This hostility to women is evidenced in many workmen's combinations elsewhere. The rules of the 'Journeymen Man Spinners, Woollen Weavers and others involved in the Woollen Trades' in Rochdale, Lancashire, in 1824 stated that 'no member of the Association shall be allowed to work at any shop where there is any woman or women weavers'. Some early English combinations accepted female members but at a lower fee of admission than men. For example the West Riding Fancy Union 'for the Protection of the Trade of Fancy Manufacture' admitted women for the same sum as that of boys under sixteen years of age, indicating that the position of women within the trade was similar to that of a male apprentice.[18] Interestingly women silk weavers in Dublin's Liberties organised an independent strike in 1825, a unique achievement in an era of male-dominated trade unionism.[19]

In the handicraft textile industries, there were many processes which involved a large amount of preparatory work before yarn was mounted on the loom, and women featured prominently in the cleaning, preparation and spinning stages.[20] In the area of silk and ribbon weaving, where less preparatory work was required, women were heavily represented in all areas of manufacture, including the actual weaving. The 1841 census indicates the breakdown of occupations in the Dublin textile trades as is shown in Table I.

Although women were strongly represented throughout the textile trades they were relatively more numerous in the ancillary branches, performing tasks which became less rewarding as the industry became more mechanised. However machine spinning in the cotton and woollen industries was introduced more slowly into Ireland than England, and so the spinning of the finer counts of yarn remained a workshop occupation for women rather longer in Dublin than in English textile towns. One mill-owner, Joseph Nicholson, believed that a major factor operating against the extension of machinery in Ireland was the low cost of labour. He wrote in 1811 that

> yarn spun by women is sold here much cheaper than the same article manufactured by machinery in England. To one unacquainted with Ireland, the smaller earnings of the poorer females - frequently not more than two pence a day...must appear very extraordinary.[21]

The abundance of cheap female labour available in the city made the very survival of female-led families precarious. With declining craft employment and probably stagnant openings in domestic service, women were over-represented among the city's unemployed and among those given charitable assistance, particularly after 1800. Workhouse numbers may not however be indicative of relative unemployment since women were more likely to seek refuge from the dangers of the city there. House of Industry and Workhouse returns show that a sizable majority of the inmates were always female, young and old.[22] Left destitute on their husbands' deaths, artisans' and even tradesmen's widows found themselves increasingly vulnerable and unemployable in a city of declining industry. The Sick and Indigent Roomkeepers' Society reported to the Poor Law Commission in 1836 that the only employment open to these women was needlework, work which was difficult to

BROPHY

TABLE I

Gender Balance in Key 'Female' Occupations
1760-1841

	1760		1800		1841		1841	
	F	M	F	M	F	M	F	M
Confectioners	0	11	12	25	24	38	194	101
Bakers	1	23	11	102	17	97	8	736
Grocers	6	195	47	263	32	377	108	439
Haberdashers	1	12	45	51	10	14	47	45
Milliners	0	5	35	0	130	4	719	0
Woollen Drapers	7	66	1	78	1	30	8	74
Linen Drapers	7	67	37	113	17	56	20	80
Glovers	1	16	2	18	1	22	248	44
Staymakers	0	24	4	10	43	4	468	2
Hatters	0	19	2	49	0	45	158	389
Upholsterers	1	5	0	1	3	109	98	90

Source: The first six columns are taken from the *Dublin Directory* of the relevant years and the figures represent the numbers of persons returned as owners of the businesses listed. The last two columns of figures represent persons involved in different levels of the trade listed in the 1841 Census and therefore include employees, apprentices etc.

procure and so badly paid that 'the most devoted labour of a female for an entire day cannot purchase a scanty meal independent of other necessities'.[23]

In the days when handicraft work had involved all the family and had been centred in the home, artisanal women had enjoyed both status within the family, and recognition as an essential source of labour. As manufacturing moved outside the home, those who continued in employment did so initially as members of the family unit; but the development of capitalism in the city's growing workshops meant that they became mere employees. As female operatives, excluded from the tradition of male collective action, they posed a threat to skilled male artisans who were becoming increasingly protective of their status in the face of employers' tendency to squeeze all wages. The result of this was that women were increasingly confined to a narrowing range of job options. As Ivy Pinchbeck has noted of English developments,

> big capitalistic production meant a division of labour in which women were relegated to certain occupations, the number of which tended to be reduced as capitalistic organisations developed.[24]

At a higher economic level the changes which forced business women out of business were as much social and cultural as they were economic. The spread of the bourgeois ethic of respectability meant that it became less acceptable for women to work without an economic need so to do. A few very profitable niches remained in the fashion clothing area, but until the openings in the new professions - such as nursing and teaching - at the end of the nineteenth century, the place of middle-class women lay outside the labour market. Their eclipse was later than for artisanal women but the rise of middle-class respectability proved for business women as confining in the long run as workplace changes were for working-class women.

NOTES

1. Sally Alexander, *Women's Work in Nineteenth-Century London, 1820-50* (London, 1976), p.33.
2. *Dublin Mercantile Advertiser*, 31 March-4 April 1767.
3. *Dublin Directory*, 1795-1805.
4. (i) *Irish Statutes 1310-1798*: 'An alledged custom in Ireland, that the testator leaving wife or child, could only dispose of half his personality by will and only one third if he left both, declared void': VIII, sect. 10, p.272; (ii) *Act for the Amendment of the Law of Inheritence*, 1833; (iii) *Act for the Amendment of the Laws with Respect to Wills*, 1837. 7 Wm.III, c.6 (1695), as summarised in *Irish Statutes* VIII, 'Wills', no. 21.
5. MS Minutes of the Dublin Society, March 1762, pp.25-8 (R.D.S. Library).
6. Ibid., pp.37-9.

7. Ada Longford, 'History of the Irish Linen and Cotton Printing Industry in the Eighteenth Century', *Journal of the Royal Society of Antiquaries of Ireland*, 5th. ser. LXVII (1937), pp.32-5.
8. Ivy Pinchbeck, *Women Workers and the Industrial Revolution 1750-1850* (London, 1969), p.287.
9. Ibid., p.289.
10. Ibid., p.223.
11. *Census of Ireland 1841*; City of Dublin Table of Occupations (Brit. Parl. Papers, 1843, XXIV).
12. *Freeman's Journal*, 3 November 1840: Report of meeting of Royal National Repeal Association.
13. Pinchbeck, *Women Workers*, pp.289-90.
14. Evidence of Richard McCormack, Worsted Manufacturer, to the Grand Committee for Trade, 1782, *House of Commons Journals (Ire.)*, X, app. cxv.
15. Fergus D'Arcy, 'Dublin Artisan Activity, Opinion and Organisation 1820-50', (unpublished U.C.D. M.A., 1968), p.16.
16. *Second Report from the Select Committee on the Combinations of Workers* (Brit. Parl. Papers, 1837-8, VIII), app. C, part II, p.341.
17. Ibid., p.345: Evidence of Mr. Morton, Shipbuilder.
18. *Report from the Select Committee on Combination Laws* (Brit. Parl. Papers, 1825, IV), p.531.
19. D'Arcy, 'Artisan Activity', p.20.
20. Pinchbeck, *Women Workers*, p.125.
21. Conrad Gill, *The Rise of the Irish Linen Industry* (Oxford, 1925), p.267.
22. *Poor Enquiry (Ireland):* App. C, pt. ii...*Dublin* (Brit. Parl. Papers, 1836, XXX), pp.21*a et seq.
23. Ibid., p.228: Evidence of Rev. T.R. Shore, Curate of St. Miehan's Parish and Secretary of the Sick and Indigent Roomkeepers' Society.
24. Pinchbeck, *Women Workers*, p.129.

APPENDIX I

The Structure of the Dublin Labour Force, 1841

SECTOR	FEMALE		MALE	
	Total Number	% of Female Labour Force	Total Number	% of Male Labour Force
1. Food Trades	1,711	4.2	5,969	9.9
2. Clothing Trades, Textiles	13,042	32.2	10,568	17.8
3. Education & Religion	763	1.9	765	1.3
4. Health	374	0.9	837	1.4
5. Justice & Police	1	0.0	3,001	5.0
6. Merchants, Shopkeepers & Assistants, Dealers & Writing Clerks	2,274	6.1	5,989	10.0
7. Construction, Furnishings, other Craft Trades & Professional Services	974	2.4	15.388	25.6
8. Servants, Labourers, Coal-porters, Chimneysweeps & Washerwomen	20,811	51.4	14,997	25.0
9. Miscellaneous	359	0.9	2,404	4.0

Source: *Census of Ireland, 1841* (Brit. Parl. Papers 1843, XXIV), p.22. The sectoral categories used here are those used in the census with the exceptions: (6) is taken from the 'Unclassified' category in the census and includes all commercial occupations listed there from 'merchants' to 'writing clerks'; (8) is taken from the 'Unclassified' and the 'Lodging' category.

CONTEMPORARY ATTITUDES TOWARDS THE HOMELESS POOR 1725 - 1775

JOSEPH O'CARROLL

By the early eighteenth century, Dublin was confronted with a serious and persistent problem of poverty. This showed itself most clearly in the great numbers of beggars and other homeless poor who 'infested' the streets and who relied almost completely on some form of material relief in order to survive. Insofar as relief existed, it came mainly in the form of private charity; however, throughout the century there were frequent calls for greater legislative control of, and more organised provision for, the homeless poor. These calls tended to ring loudest during periods of crisis but the issue was always topical and gradually a somewhat more sophisticated attitude developed towards the whole phenomenon of poverty. Here the intention is to explore the ways in which contemporary perceptions and analyses of poverty informed the actual measures taken to solve the problem of the homeless poor between the 1720s and the 1770s.

Contrary to first appearances, the poor of eighteenth-century Dublin did not constitute a single homogeneous entity. Contemporary observers showed their awareness of this by applying various criteria to distinguish the different categories. The primary distinction was between *strange* and *local* beggars; this had first been legally recognised in Ireland in 1542 in the

statute of 33 Hen. VIII, c.15. The act was an almost verbatim
extension of the English act restricting vagabonds, passed
eleven years previously, which had authorised Justices of the
Peace and mayors to issue letters of registration to 'aged and
impotent persons subsisting by alms', permitting them to beg
within their own districts. Sixty years later the parish system
was further strengthened in England by the act of 43 Elizabeth
I, c.2. which made compulsory the levying of a rate in each
parish for the maintenance of its own poor. This was to form
the basis of the English poor-law system until 1834, when the
indoor relief and workhouse system came into operation.
Unfortunately the Elizabethan act was never extended to
Ireland, with the result that poor people were unlikely to
receive alms in their own localities. It was partly as a result of
this that in Ireland those in distress continued to take to the road
- during the bad years in vast numbers - in search of food or
work, beginning a journey which, according to Dean Swift,
nearly always led to Dublin.[1] In gravitating towards the city the
rural poor merely reflected and were possibly encouraged by
the centrality of the capital which 'drew a constant resort of
people from all parts of the island'.[2] It was not only food and
money which attracted them; two women, Dorothy King and
Mary Johnson, both from Cork and both pregnant, were
maintained during confinement by St. Michan's parish vestry
in 1729 and later given money to return home. Between
October 1728 and July 1729, the parish made eight other
payments to strangers to help them return to their place of
origin, although whether the money was actually used for this
purpose is debatable.[3] Certainly such payments served to
convince the rural poor, as Swift put it, that 'money, as they
perceive, always abounds in the metropolis'.[4]

   This general propensity among the poor to gravitate towards
the city was heightened in years of crop failure or other rural
economic crisis - such as the later 1720s and the 1760s. It is no
coincidence that the bulk of Swift's writings on the question of
poverty appeared between 1725 and 1735 or that the Dublin
'House of Industry' was erected in the early 1770s. Between
these two severe decades there were other crises, much the

most serious being that of 1740-41: it seems that up to 8,000
people per day were being 'relieved' in Dublin in the summer
of 1741,[5] three to four times the 'normal' population of street
beggars.[6]

There was also a recurring seasonal factor in rural poverty.
Arthur Dobbs estimated in 1731 that for every ten who lived on
alms throughout the whole year, there were thirty who 'shut up
their doors and go a begging the whole summer until harvest,
with their wives and children'.[7] These, he maintained, usually
farmed the poorer land in mountainous areas. The likelihood is
that while good weather lasted, it made more sense for the rural
poor to live on charity in the city than to consume any part of
the meagre resources upon which they relied for subsistence
for the other eight or nine months of the year.

Not surprisingly, the citizens of Dublin had little or no
sympathy for the 'foreign' poor. While they were willing to
extend relief to their own beggars, they baulked at the idea of
supporting those from the countryside of Leinster and beyond.
A solution to the problem of distinguishing between the *strange*
and the *local* poor was seen to lie in a system of badging or
licensing, originally suggested by the Henrician act. Given that
the parish authorities were familiar with their own poor, it was
thought that if they distributed badges to the paupers of the
parish and confined them to beg within their own parishes, any
'strangers' could easily be apprehended. Swift claimed that he
never heard more than one objection to this: 'what shall we do
with the foreign beggars?'[8] Echoing the Henrician act he
suggested that they

> be driven or whipped out of the town [and sent] from one parish to
> another until they reach their own homes, [for by] the old laws of
> England still in force, and I presume by those in Ireland, every parish is
> bound to maintain its own poor.[9]

It would seem that while Swift was familiar with both the
Henrician and the Elizabethan acts, he wrongly assumed that
both had been extended to Ireland, when in fact this was only
true in the case of the former. In Ireland, the parishes were not
bound to support their own poor and this in turn was bound to
make any system of parish badging in Dublin almost

The City Workhouse, 1728 (detail from Charles Broking, *Map of the City and Suburbs of Dublin*...(London, 1728))

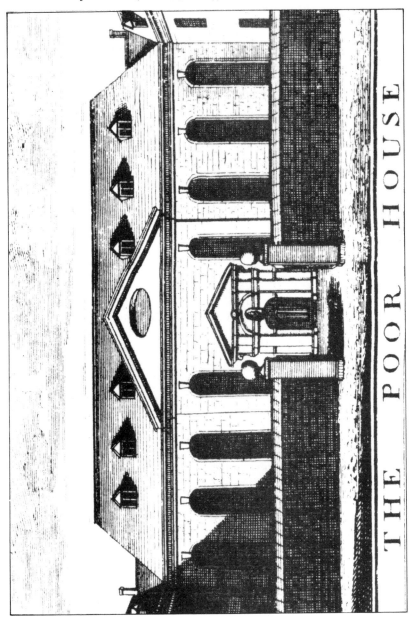

unworkable. Strangers could be driven out of a city parish but there was nothing to prevent their coming back. In order to counteract the itinerant tendencies of the poor, it would have been necessary to apply the same system throughout the country.

There were also other impediments to badging which prevented its successful application even in Dublin. Opposition came from the beggars themselves. Not surprisingly they actively resisted the kind of control over their movements that badging entailed: 'they are too lazy to work, they are not afraid to steal, nor ashamed to beg; and yet are too proud to be seen with a badge' claimed Swift.[10] Sir William Fownes, the lord mayor of Dublin in 1708-09, noted in 1725 that

> unless it [badging] be done effectually, and frequent reviews taken, vagabonds and cheats will find ways to buy or hire badges, or get counterfeits; and it is to be suspected that the badged poor will shelter and connive with strange beggars if not put under some penalty when discovered.[11]

A year later, the archbishop of Dublin, William King, directed his clergy to carry out such a badging operation; however it 'proved wholly ineffectual, [owing to]...the fraud, perverseness and pride of the said poor'.[12]

A further impediment to effective badging was the corruption of the parish beadles, or 'bellowers' as they were known, whose job it was to control the beggars. In 1723 the Irish statute book recorded

> that great numbers of idle and vagrant persons do daily resort from the country to the city of Dublin and the suburbs thereof, who by reason of the correspondence they do generally keep with the beadles of the several parishes, and the neglect of such beadles in the performance of their duties, are permitted to beg in and through the city.[13]

Fourteen years later Swift said that when he mentioned the problem to any minister of a city parish, the latter 'usually lays the fault upon the beadles who are bribed by the foreign beggars and [who] often keep ale-houses', where the beggars were good customers.[14] During the crisis of 1766 the Lord Mayor, Edward Sankey, issued a proclamation that all unbadged beggars be rounded up.[15] The following year a reward of 2s.6d. for each beggar apprehended was offered because, 'owing to the negligence of the constables, beadles and other parish officers', the first proclamation had proved ineffectual.[16] The number of unbadged beggars does not appear to have been diminished by these steps and this, together with the agitation of several prominent individuals notably Dean Richard Woodward, led to new measures being introduced in 1771 to deal with the problem.

The act of 11&12 Geo. III, c.30 established county and city 'corporations' to oversee the badging of the poor and the erection of 'houses of industry' for the incarceration of those who were unlicensed. Between November 1773 and March 1775, 970 badges were issued in Dublin and 1,338 people taken into the House.[17] This new threat to the 'foreign' beggars seems to have had the desired effect. Woodward observed that they 'either withdrew from the city or betook themselves to useful industry'.[18] The problem of the 'foreign' poor seemed to have been solved for the moment.

Another long-established distinction that was used to identify different types of poor was that between the 'impotent poor' - those physically unable to work who could not survive without relief - and the 'sturdy poor' - those who, it was believed, took advantage of charity in order to avoid having to work; all able-bodied unemployed adult males were subsumed within this category. Contemporary estimates were that the 'sturdy poor' formed between 85 per cent to 95 per cent of the total. Swift, as usual, provided the harshest assessment, maintaining that

> among the meaner people, nineteen in twenty of those who are reduced to a starving condition did not become so by the work of God, either upon their bodies or their goods.[19]

At about the same time Arthur Dobbs suggested that of the 34,000 beggars in the whole country, 30,000 were capable of working, a proportion of 87 per cent.[20] About forty years later Woodward estimated, that the 'average number of sick [poor] amounts to upwards of one-tenth,[21] therefore leaving 90 per cent sturdy. On the other hand William Fownes had commented in 1725 that

> it is very usual to hear people cry out, why are not the beggars taken
> up and sent to workhouses, little considering how few of such beggars
> are able to do any work.[22]

It is likely in fact that the relative sizes of the two groups
fluctuated considerably depending on conditions, but we can
assume that the 'sturdy poor' would have made up the great
majority except during severe epidemic crises, such as that of
1740-41; at these times even the 'sturdy poor' would have been
quickly exposed to the contagion.

There was little or no sympathy for the community of
beggars, whose dominant characteristics were always assumed
to be 'idleness, drunkenness, thievery and cheating'. The chief
solution to the menace they represented was the creation of
correctional institutions which would inculcate into them the
habit of industriousness. The view of poverty as a kind of
moral malaise curable by the discipline of hard work was a
conventional wisdom, current far beyond the confines of
eighteenth-century Dublin; it provided the ideological basis for
the establishment of both the Workhouse and the House of
Industry, the names of which are largely explanatory of their
purpose.

The first Dublin Workhouse had been established in 1703 by
the act of 2 Anne, c.19, as a means of controlling the sturdy
poor. However by 1725 almost half the inmates were children
and all but seven of the adults were deemed incapable of
working. The Workhouse also took on a national character
from the outset, even though it was financed by a tax levied on
Dublin households alone. In a typically swingeing attack, Swift
charged that

> as the whole fund for supporting this hospital is raised only from the
> inhabitants of the city, so there can hardly be anything more absurd
> than to see it mis-employed in maintaining foreign beggars and
> bastards.[23]

By 1750 it had become almost exclusively a 'foundling
hospital', its original purpose defeated by a combination of bad
management, inadequate finances, the even more pressing
problem of deserted children, and the understandable reluctance
of the sturdy beggars to relinquish their freedom. To combat

this latter problem it would have been necessary to create some form of special municipal police for apprehending the beggars - and indeed this was done seventy years later when the House of Industry came into operation. In the later 1770s the 'black cart' with its armed beadles became a familiar sight in the city's streets as it set out in pursuit of sturdy beggars.[24] Of the 1,138 taken into the House of Industry between 1773 and 1775, 742 were brought in under duress;[25] from descriptions of the open street warfare that broke out from time to time it seems likely that hundreds more managed to escape the dragnet.[26]

One of the most surprising aspects of the situation after 1750 is that in the twenty-year period between the total abandonment of the original function of the Workhouse and the creation of the House of Industry the city possessed no correctional institution for beggars. The only alternative was the prisons which were already overcrowded and which could not provide the 'sturdy poor' with work, the reason for their incarceration.[27] In 1766 the Corporation heard that while many such persons had been committed to the Bridewell, 'for want of proper employment, the purpose of their confinement was not answered'.[28] It is likely that the committee set up to investigate this situation, led by the previously mentioned Lord Mayor, Edward Sankey, played a major role in the process which culminated in the erection of the House of Industry.[29]

Dublin Corporation's concern over the issue was based on the assumption that there was a strong relationship between poverty and crime. This belief had been reinforced by the apparent concurrence of high food prices and urban crime waves. Thus in January 1740, at the height of the great frost which brought on the health crisis of the following two years, it was noted in *Faulkner's Dublin Journal* that 'there are more house-breakers and street-robbers in and about the city now, than ever was known in this kingdom'.[30] In June of the same year the Corporation was

> greatly disturbed by numbers of idle and disorderly persons assembling themselves in many parts [of the city] who violently broke open the houses of several of the inhabitants and forcibly removed their goods.[31]

Other newspaper reports confirm that this was in fact a bread riot.[32]

In 1753, Henry Fielding's influential pamphlet, *An Inquiry into the Causes of the late Increase of Robbers...*, originally published in London, was reprinted in Dublin; it sought to demonstrate a definite link between crime and poverty. And the combined effects of the crises of 1757, 1763-64, and 1766-67 seem to have further increased the public awareness of the link. In the hard year of 1766 the Lord Mayor, William Forbes,

> pulled down a notorious bull-yard at the corner of Aungier St. and York St. which was represented to him by the principle inhabitants as a great nuisance to the neighbourhood, by breaking their windows, cursing, swearing and all manner of vice, that a place frequented by profligate vagabonds was capable of.[33]

Such places were quite common around the city and the Corporation was constantly hearing similar complaints. How far the opening of the House of Industry reduced the level of crime is an open question. Woodward claimed in 1775 that the 'suppression of begging has checked the illegal combinations of journeymen',[34] although the fact that he was trying to raise fresh donations for the House of Industry may have led him to make exaggerated claims.

Besides crime, there was drink: official concern was repeatedly expressed over the 'extravagant drunkenness' of the 'sturdy poor'. Swift complained that they would not accept alms in the form of food or clothes but wanted only money which they needed to buy 'ale, brandy and other strong liquors'.[35] In 1770 John Rutty, the Quaker doctor, provided an excellent description of the situation:

> whiskey among the lower ranks has for some years so enormously prevailed, not only to the corrupting of the morals and destroying of the constitutions of the drinkers, even of both sexes, but to the debasing and enfeebling of their progeny...[36]

One of the benefits of the House of Industry, as cited by Woodward, was that it effected a 'reduction in the number of low retailers of spirituous liquors'[37] who catered for this great demand. Rutty stated that from a 'computation' made in 1749 there were at least 3,500 alehouses, taverns and brandyshops in the city, one for about every thirty inhabitants (including children).[38] This does not include the illegal street-vendors of alcohol who were reportedly also very numerous.[39] It may well be that alcohol acted as an appetite suppressant where people's diets were deficient, although no doubt its intoxicating quality was the main reason for its popularity, even among beggars.

Given this situation one might expect that sickness would have been more widespread among the poor, but as we have seen, during normal times the sick probably made up only 5 to 15 per cent of the street poor. It is likely of course that the sick poor were elsewhere, being the first to be institutionalised, the easiest to apprehend and the most likely to die when they became ill. Such factors may account for the relatively small proportion of the 'impotant poor' in contemporary estimates. It is possible to gain some insight into the ailments which afflicted this group. In Marsh's Library a classified list of all those in the Workhouse in 1725 survives from which the following tables are derived. (A comparison of the style and content with Fownes' publication of the same year would suggest that he was also responsible for the document).

Some attempts were made to treat the poor on the basis of their ailments. Swift's bequest for the establishment of a hospital for the insane is well known. The need for this was obvious: of those held in the Workhouse in 1725, the three groups listed as 'madd', 'fools', and 'has fitts', make up 14.8 per cent of the total. If the healthy children and adults are excluded from the inmate total, this proportion rises to over 30 per cent. Indeed the presence of insane people in the Workhouse caused considerable concern to the governors and this was echoed in the early parliamentary reports, as was the fact that so many of the inmates were incapable of working.

The concern to make particular provision for the sick poor is one of the more discernible features of eighteenth-century attitudes. Besides St. Patrick's Hospital, established under the terms of Swift's will, there were also a number of institutions catering for the 'sick and wounded' or the 'incurables', which were maintained by private charity. Indeed the period between 1725 and 1775 marked a high point in the foundation of what

TABLE I

Medico-social Status of Dublin Workhouse
Inmates, 1725

MS Classification	No.	Per Cent	Mean Age
'Superannuate'	30	13.5	
'Infirm'	26	11.7	63
'Bed-rid'	7	3.2	
'Madd'	16	7.2	
'Fooles'	14	6.3	29
'Has fitts'	3	1.4	
'Kings evil' (scrofula)	6	2.7	
'Blind'	9	4.1	
'Dumb'	4	1.8	
'Lame'	7	3.2	
Healthy Adults	7	3.2	
Healthy Children	93	41.9	

Source: 'A List of the Poor in the City Workhouse, from the Several Parishes with their Age and Qualities, March 20th. 1725', (Marsh's Library, MS 2.3.1. [1], cxlv-viii).

TABLE II

Composition of Workhouse Inmates by Sex and Age, 1725

Sex	No.	Per Cent	Average Age
Males/Adult	46	20.7	50
Females/Adult	66	29.7	52
Males/Children	53	23.8	9
Females/Children	57	25.8	10.5

Source: As for Table I.

were later termed 'voluntary' hospitals.

The primary motive leading the wealthy citizenry to make special provision for the poor was their fear of contagious disease. Swift noted that 'a famine among the poor has often been the occasion of pestilential and contagious distempers, whereby the rich become sharers in the general calamity'.[40] The terrible typhus and dysentery epidemics of 1740-1 once again acted to sharpen public consciousness, as infections which originally moved among the poor spread to even the most exclusive households. The possibility of infection was a recurring fear among the wealthy citizens of the city. For instance in 1745 a newspaper report mentioned that 'several persons ill of the small-pox have of late been exposed in the most frequented parts of the city...to the terror of several of the inhabitants'.[41] Often there was a tendency to treat all beggars as disease-ridden , a fact which no doubt acted to their advantage when soliciting for alms.

Another criteria used to categorise the poor was age. There were three broad categories: children under the age of six, children between the ages of six and fifteen, and those over fifteen.[42] Without doubt children were the main objects of relief, both private and institutional, and there was a large number of organisations set up for the purposes of educating and controlling poor children. It was thought that if children could be caught early enough it would be possible to change their moral habits and make them responsible and industrious, so preventing the development of another generation of beggars.[43] There was also a major proselytising element in the education of Catholic children. In 1733 the Incorporated Society for Promoting English Protestant Schools was set up in Dublin with the specific aim of converting poor Catholic children. Those in the Workhouse and Foundling Hospital were also supposed to receive instruction from Church of Ireland clergy but, in practice, this was seldom the case. Most parishes had a charity school attached to the church, where children were taught to work and given a rudimentary education in numeracy before being placed in apprenticeships or domestic service under Protestant employers. By these

means it was hoped that the perennial problem of dishonest
servants would be circumvented. The Corporation's 'Blue-
Coat School' in Queen St. established in 1670 as 'a place of
abode for the...relief of poor children, aged, maimed and
impotent people inhabiting the city of Dublin' had by the mid-
eighteenth century become exclusively a school for the sons of
poorer Protestant citizens.[44] Complementary to this, a school
for the children of soldiers was opened in the city in 1767 and
another for the children of 'decayed' seamen in 1773 - in order
to protect such children from 'the evils of popery, beggary and
idleness', upon the death or enforced absence of their parents.[45]
There was always great concern about the bad influences that
the young would be exposed to if allowed to go unsupervised.
Fownes commented that 'there are numbers of those straggling
about [who] pretend to live by selling newspapers, blacking of
shoes and running often on pimping errands from taverns';[46]
many of these were sent from the country or were unemployed
apprentices, and Fownes claimed that that they were
'notoriously wicked and ought to be confined to
Workhouses'.[47]

The biggest problem of all was the huge number of
foundlings. The practice of abandoning children was
widespread among the poorer sections of society. Often girls
from the country would pay a visit to the city to dispose of their
unwanted offspring, while those from the city would seek out a
distant parish to 'drop' theirs. One of the functions of the
beadles was to discover the mothers of deserted children for
which a reward of 10s.10d. per discovery was offered.
Notwithstanding this reward the rate of success does not seem
to have been very high, even though the beadles of different
parishes co-operated in the task of discovery.[48] The parish
vestries were reluctant to accept responsibility for deserted
children, which led to the practice of 'dropping' or 'lifting'
them from one parish to another. Country parishes often paid
to have their foundlings brought up in the city and 'dropped'
there in bulk. Eventually in 1727 the act of 1 Geo.II, c.27
bound the parish vestries to care for these children, the extra
finance to come from a new cess of 3d. in the rateable value of

each house. However this proved such a burden that three years later it was decided that all such foundlings would be taken into the city Workhouse, the name of which was changed to the Foundling Hospital and Workhouse of the City of Dublin. This act of 3 Geo.II, c.17 suspended for two years the original 3d. tax that had been initiated in 1727, while imposing another one for an equal amount in order to create extra finance for the Workhouse.

There was no obvious improvement in the lot of the foundlings. Between 1735 and 1743, 3,972 foundlings were admitted into the Workhouse of whom 2,754 later died.[49] This level of mortality has led modern writers to the conclusion that the Foundling Hospital was a failure, but the fact is that the principal object of the system was not to protect the foundlings and ensure that they were kept in good health - an almost impossible task given their usual condition on admittance - but rather to remove them from the streets and the parishes where they created a nuisance. The greatest concern was with the cost of the operation, and the board of governors of the Workhouse/Foundling Hospital seem to have turned a blind eye to the situation as long as it did not constitute too much of a financial burden.

The generally high awareness of the specific problem of the young and very young was matched by a great ignorance of, or at least indifference towards, the equally obvious problem of the old. The average age of adults incarcerated in the Workhouse in 1725 was 51 years. Of the three groups listed as 'superannuate', 'bed-ridden' and 'infirm', the average age was 63 years. If the three groups earlier described as insane or mentally handicapped, who had an average age of 29 years and made up 30 per cent of the total sick, are excluded, then the average age of the remaining adults was over 60 years. Much the same was true of those in the House of Industry fifty years later: of the 1,338 taken in between 1773 and 1775, 728, or 55 per cent, were also over 60 years of age.[50] This would seem to indicate that a large proportion of the 'impotent poor' were suffering from no more than old age and its attendant problems. However, while there were occasional references to the 'aged poor', no attempt was made to provide separate provision for them.

Other criteria which were used to distinguish the poor were sex and religion. Swift noted in his *Modest Proposal* and elsewhere that it was 'beggars of the female sex' who predominated on the streets, accompanied by their children.[51] Both he and Fownes maintained that many of these hired additional children to assist in their appeals.[52] Dobbs painted a terrible picture, stating that

> they exercise the greatest barbarities upon children, either their own or those they pick up, by blinding them, or breaking and disjointing their limbs when they are young, to make them objects of compassion and charity.[53]

Evidence from Protestant parish registers tends to confirm the over-representation of women among those forced to beg; the registers record that widows were often completely reduced to destitution by the death of their husbands, and widows-houses were usually maintained by the vestries, sometimes in the same building as the parish charity school.[54] And in the Workhouse in 1725, there were 66 females as opposed to 46 males; in the House of Industry during 1775 the proportions were 760 women to 578 men.[55]

Religious considerations were evident in all eighteenth-century thinking on the subject of poverty and its relief. As has been shown in the case of children, much of this was inspired by the proselytising drive. Often the charitable bequests entrusted to parish vestries specified that the recipients be Protestants. For example, in 1749 Charles Powel left a total of £3,000 to be shared out among ten parishes. Of this £1,000 was to be spent on apprenticing 20 poor boys to Protestant tradesmen, the rest to be invested and the interest used for the relief of 'ten decayed protestants' in each parish;[56] in 1775 £20 was bequeathed to 'poor protestant roomkeepers' in St. Andrew's.[57] It would seem that, in general, Protestant parishioners had first claim on the funds available for relief - which were never enough to satisfy demand. On the other hand, there was considerably less emphasis placed on religion by the authorities at the Workhouse and House of Industry. As with the parish charity schools, the official intention was that the children be apprenticed to Protestant tradesmen, but this hardly ever happened. Possibly the area of most controversy was the practice of using 'Papist' nurses to wean infant foundlings. There were continual complaints about this on the grounds that it contradicted the whole idea of giving charity. But there was no room in the Workhouse and it was in any case cheaper to maintain the foundlings outside, so nothing was done to end the practice. Given the circumstances, religion was set aside by practical considerations. The likelihood is that the majority of the homeless who received relief at any stage were Catholic; this must certainly have been the case with the poor who came from the country.

Eighteenth-century observers of the Dublin poor had therefore a relatively sophisticated set of attitudes towards the problem of poverty; derivative in certain respects, their ideas were informed by local observation and reflected the situation on the ground. Rather than simply treating the poor as an amorphous mass of degenerate humanity, they attempted to devise specific responses to the different types of pauper which they perceived to exist. The distinctions they made were broadly based on origin, physical and mental health, ability to work, age, sex and religion, and within these categories they further distinguished sub-groups. They also isolated a direct link between poverty and such social problems as crime, drunkenness and contagious disease. As far as the effects of poverty were concerned, contemporaries harboured few illusions. The motivation underlying their attempts to solve the pauper problem was only slightly tinged by humanitarian feelings. It was pragmatic considerations which influenced their attitudes, and particularly the twin threats posed by excessive vagrancy - the breakdown of law and order on the streets, and the challenge to public health. Hence social policy aimed at greater control rather than greater care of the homeless poor - badging and enforced work in the case of the sturdy, removal from public view and circulation in the case of foundlings and the sick. The old, who posed little danger, were almost completely ignored as a result.

It was in the analysis of causation that the most interesting developments in thinking took place. Traditionally poverty was seen as resulting from the inherent qualities of the individual, variously expressed in terms of moral degeneracy, indolence, or simply laziness. According to this view it was primarily the fault of a person's nature if he or she was poor. In addition all Catholics, shackled by a morally inferior religion, tended towards laziness and therefore poverty. As the century progressed, these views began to be challenged. Swift, who never completely abandoned a moral view, was nonetheless one of the first to posit an alternative. In 1724 he wrote that 'trade is the only incitement to labour; where that fails the poorer native must either beg, steal or starve, or be forced to quit his country'.[58] He bemoaned the fact that children were 'brought up to steal or beg, for want of work'.[59] Two years later in an implied critique of traditional ideas, he admitted that 'we are apt to charge the Irish with laziness, because we seldom find them employed, but then we don't consider [that] they have nothing to do'.[60] Three years later Thomas Prior, in his *List of Absentees,* noted that 'people, who are willing to support themselves by their labour, are left to struggle with poverty, for want of employment'.[61] In Swift's view, the irresponsibility of rural landlords, failing to develop their estates and deal equitably with their tenants, contributed substantially to the influx of 'foreign' beggars into Dublin.[62] For both Swift and Prior the spending of Irish rents abroad led to a shortage of specie at home and ultimately to unemployment. By 1735 Berkeley had developed the argument further, querying whether

> the industry of the people is not to be considered as that which constitutes wealth, which makes even land and silver to be wealth, neither of which would have any value but as means and motive to industry.[63]

Indeed, Berkeley's famous work, the *Querist* , had originally sprung from an 'urgent, pressing problem of unemployment and poverty'.[64]

This understanding of poverty as a condition which was brought about by factors over which the poor had no control was in turn reflected in the development of a new attitude to relief. The first explicit Irish statement of this was in Richard Woodward's *Argument in Support of the Right of the Poor...to a National Provision,* published in 1768. It is worth noting that Woodward was at that stage rector of St. Werburgh's parish as well as dean of Clogher; he spent much of his time in the city. In the course of the pamphlet he claimed that the poor had a right to be relieved, since it was not their fault that they were so reduced. Indeed, he continued, to give such relief was the duty of the wealthy and if it were not forthcoming then the poor could not be blamed for withdrawing their loyalty to the state. In constructing his argument he rejected the Lockean concept that civil society is based on a contractual relationship between the individual and government.

However, it would be a mistake to see the new political economy or Woodward's political enlightenment as heralding any kind of breakthrough in the general attitudes of the propertied classes. Calls for drastic new measures to relieve the homeless poor invariably involved parliamentary or parochial involvement in an area which would have proven prohibitively costly in terms of new taxation. In Dublin the experience of the Workhouse was enough to convince people that this would be the case. The great expense and gross mismanagement of that institution had resulted in parliamentary enquiries in 1725, 1737, 1743, 1758, 1760, 1764, 1767 and 1775.[65] The Workhouse had cost the huge sum of £9,000 to construct and the original intention had been that it should be financed by a wide range of taxes.[66] These included levies on the yearly licences of hackney cars, brewers' drays, sedan chairs and all commercial carts as well as a rate of 3d. in the pound on the value of every house in the city and liberties. Given such revenues it might have been expected that the Workhouse would pay for itself, especially in light of the fact that its income was supposed to be supplemented by the productive work of its inmates. But the Workhouse was in fact in debt from the beginning. By 1752 the governors had begun regularly to petition Parliament for aid. In that year £1,000 was

granted [67] and in the following year, another £2,000.[68] In 1755
they were refused a grant, and a petition by the 'merchants and
others' of the city calling for an investigation into the
misapplication of funds was lodged.[69] Nonetheless in 1756
£4,000 was granted (at the same time Mercer's hospital
received £500, St. Patricks £1,000 and the new Lying-In
Hospital £6,000 to cover its opening - all supposedly voluntary
hospitals supported by charity).[70] It took another 15 years and a
decade of severe crises before the nettle was grasped again.
The new House of Industry, which opened in 1772, operated
under the statute of 11&12 Geo.III, c.30, but it was to be
voluntarily funded. The fear of an uncontrollable poor tax was
a recurring nightmare for propertied citizens. It is significant
that seven years after Woodward had asserted the 'rights' of
the poor he chose to beat an intellectual retreat. When seeking
donations to the House of Industry in 1775, he appealed
'solely to the interests' of his readers.[71] By pointing to

> the perpetual interruption of the business of the shop-keeper, the
> inconvenience of the passenger, the horror and danger of exposing
> loathsome, infectious and frightful objects in the street, and the
> consequent disgrace to the police,

he was probably more likely to produce the desired monetary
response than by exploring the radical territory of social
responsibility.[72]

NOTES

1.   J. Swift, 'A Proposal for Giving Badges to the Beggars of Dublin',
      in *Prose Works of Swift*, VII (London, 1925), p.328.
2.   'A Description of the City of Dublin by a Citizen of London', in
      Sir John Gilbert (ed.), *Calendar of the Ancient Records of Dublin*,
      X, p.519.
3.   W. O'Brien, 'St. Michan's Parish, 1724-1775: A Study in Local
      Government' (unpublished B.A. (Mod) dissertation, T.C.D., 1983),
      p.72.
4.   Swift, op. cit., p.334.
5.   *Pue's Occurences*, 10-14 March 1740/1.

6. R. Woodward, *An Address to the Public on the Expediency of a Regular Plan for the Maintenance and Government of the Poor* (Dublin, 1775), p.22.
7. A. Dobbs, *An Essay on the Trade of Ireland* (Dublin, 1731), II, p.47.
8. Swift, op. cit., p.316.
9. Ibid., p.329.
10. Ibid.
11. W. Fownes, *Methods Proposed for Regulating the Poor* (Dublin, 1725), p.4.
12. J. Swift, 'Letter to the Archbishop of Dublin, Dr. King, 26 September, 1726', in *Prose Works of Swift*, op. cit., p.327.
13. 10 Geo.I, c.3.
14. Swift, op.cit., p.323.
15. *C.A.R.D.*, XI, p.523.
16. Ibid., p.525.
17. F.S. Flood, 'Report upon Vagrancy and Mendicity in the City of Dublin', in *Poor Enquiry (Irl.)*, App. C, part ii (Brit. Parl. Papers, 1836, XXX), p.18a.
18. Woodward, op. cit., p.22.
19. Swift, op. cit., p.330.
20. Dobbs, op. cit., p.46.
21. Woodward, op. cit. p.19.
22. Fownes, op. cit., p.6.
23. Swift, op. cit., p.326.
24. T. King Moylan, 'Vagabonds and Sturdy Beggars', in *Dublin Historical Record*, I, 3 (1938), 48.
25. Flood, op. cit., p.18a.
26. Moylan, op. cit., pp.48-49.
27. See below, chapters by B. Doorley and D. Kelly.
28. *C.A.R.D.*, XI, p.327.
29. Ibid., pp.327-28.
30. *Faulkner's Dublin Journal*, no. 1413, 22 December 1739-6 January 1740, p.2.
31. *C.A.R.D.*, VIII, p.375.
32. *Faulkner's Dublin Journal*, no. 1450, 31 May-3 June 1740, p.2.
33. *C.A.R.D.*, XIII, p.328.
34. Woodward, op. cit., p.11.
35. Swift, op. cit., p.334.
36. J. Rutty, *Natural History of Dublin* (Dublin, 1772), p.12.
37. Woodward, op. cit., p.16.

38. Rutty, op. cit., p.13.

39. O'Brien, op. cit., p.63.

40. J. Swift, 'The Memorial of the Poor Inhabitants, Tradesmen and Labourers of the Kingdom of Ireland', in H. Davis (ed.), *Swift's Irish Tracts 1728-1733* (Oxford, 1955), p.303.

41. *Faulkner's Dublin Journal*, no. 1923, 6 August - 10 August 1745, p.4.

42. These were by no means rigid. At times different age parametres were used. Adults in the House of Industry were further sub-divided into under 30 years, 30-60 years and over 60 years.

43. J. Swift, 'Causes of the Wretched Condition of Ireland', in Louis London (ed.), *Irish Tracts and Sermons* (Oxford, 1968), p.207.

44. J. Warburton, J. Whitelaw and R. Walsh, *History of the City of Dublin* (Dublin, 1818), I, 565.

45. Ibid., p.602.

46. Fownes, op. cit., p.9.

47. Ibid.

48. O'Brien, op.cit., p.74.

49. 'Report from the Committee...[on the] Workhouse', *H. of C. Journals (Ire.)*, IV, app. clxxiv.

50. Flood, op. cit., p.18a.

51. J. Swift, 'A Modest Proposal for Preventing the Children of Poor People From Being a Burden', in T. Scott (ed.), *The Prose Works of Jonathan Swift* (London, 1725), p.321.

52. Fownes, op. cit., p.9.

53. Dobbs, op. cit., p.45.

54. W. Monck Mason, 'Notes on the Vestry Books of St. Andrew's Parish', T.C.D. MSS. 2062-3.

55. Flood, op. cit., p.18a.

56. Monck Mason, op. cit., p.121.

57. Ibid., p.125.

58. J. Swift, 'The Truth of some Maxims in State and Government Examined with Reference to Ireland', in *Prose Works*, op. cit., p.70.

59. Ibid., p.71.

60. J. Swift, 'The Present Miserable State of Ireland', in *Prose Works*, op. cit., p.164.

61. Cited in P. Kelly, 'Ireland and the Critique of Mercantilism in Berkeley's "Querist" ', in *Hermathema*, CXXXIX (1985), 107.

62. Swift, 'Considerations About Maintaining the Poor' in *Prose Works*, op. cit., p.341. Also, 'Maxims' in *Prose Works*, op.cit., pp.69-71, and 'Modest Proposal', in *Prose Works*, op. cit., p. 329.

63. G. Berkeley, 'The Querist' in George Sampson (ed.), *The Works of George Berkeley* (London, 1898), 435, query no. 40.

64. Kelly, op. cit., 101.

65. *H. of C. Journals (Ire.)* III, pp. 423-30, app. cccxxii; IV, app. clxxiv; VI, app. xcvi, ccccxiv; VII, app. cccxvi; VIII, clxi; IX, app. cccxcii.

66. 2 Anne c.19; Flood, op. cit., p.17a.

67. *H. of C. Journals (Ire.)*, V, p.132.

68. Ibid., pp.185-6.

69. Ibid., p.244.

70. Ibid., p.390.

71. Woodward, op. cit., p. 7.

72. Ibid., p.12.

The Potato Lady, *circa* 1775 (*J.R.S.A.I.*, 5th. ser. (1925),).

THE PARISH POOR OF
ST. MARK'S

RUTH LAVELLE
AND
PAUL HUGGARD

The parish of St. Mark's 'abounds with narrow streets, lanes, yards...of the most filthy and revolting description...a vast number depend on their daily labour for support, and many are in want of immediate relief...'.[1] The south-quayside parish, so described in 1833, had always had its social problems. As a civic and ecclesiastical unit, it had been created in 1708 out of part of the old St. Andrew's parish, a move made necessary by growth of new streets adjacent to Trinity College. St. Mark's boundaries covered the region bounded by the Liffey, Westmoreland Street, Nassau Street, Leinster Street, Fenian Street, Grand Canal Street and South Lotts Road. In Whitelaw's 1798 census of the city, 8,692 persons were located in the parish, the seventh largest of the city's 21 parishes.[2] On the face of it, the density of population in the parish, 146 per acre, was by no means as great as in some of the smaller inner-city parishes (St. Michan's beside Christ Church had 439 persons per acre according to Whitelaw),[3] but St. Mark's had within it the ample university site which distorts the density measure. A clearer indication of social conditions in the parish was the average number of inhabitants per house, which Whitelaw reckoned to be 13.45. This was one of the highest in the city, exceeded only by St. Catherine's (13.62), St. John's (14.08), St. Michan's (15.94) and the worst, St.

Luke's in the Liberties (15.95).[4] The parish was however, one of social contrast; a dock-side neighbourhood with a small university precinct bordering some of the most wealthy households in the city on the Dawson and Molesworth estates. Already by 1798, the work of the Wide Streets Commissioners in opening up the area south and south-east of the new Carlisle Bridge (i.e. the modern O'Connell Bridge) had dramatically upgraded the western edge of the parish. Whitelaw enumerated 1,283 'upper and middle class' residents in the parish, who housed 475 servants and doubtless gave employment to far more; the remaining 80 per cent, 6,924 persons, made up 'the lower classes'.[5]

St. Mark's poorer back alleys were as squalid as any Whitelaw encountered on his censal enquiries and were recorded in his vivid prose:

> As I was usually out at very early hours on the survey I have frequently surprised from ten to sixteen persons of all ages and sexes, in a room, not fifteen feet square, stretched on a wad of filthy straw, swarming with vermin.[6]

In a parish poor list for 1800, the majority of the 90 names listed come from the following streets - Townsend Street, Park Place, Poolbeg Street, Moss Street, Stocking Lane, White's Lane, Gloster Street, Boyne Street, Fleet Street, Tennis Court, Hawkins Street, Aston Quay and George's Quay. Thus there were paupers both in the main streets of the parish and in the small side streets and alleys. From the printed schedules in Whitelaw's census, we know that *house* occupancy rates were highest on the quays (18.2 persons per house) and lowest in the side streets (11.7 persons per house); this however reflects house size rather than social conditions (see Appendix I). We can assume that in the area between the river and the university, *room* occupancy rates were high, even by Dublin's claustrophobic standards.

*   *   *

The parish vestry, the assembly of male householders convened by the Church of Ireland parish officials, had by the

Bird's Eye View of St. Mark's Parish, 1846 (detail from *View of Dublin*, 1846).

eighteenth century become one of the main components of civic government in Dublin. The general vestry meeting was an annual affair, open to dissenters and Catholics as well as members of the Established Church, but the many administrative functions performed under the authority of the vestry were in fact overseen and regulated by a much smaller group of active, propertied Church of Ireland citizens, whether informally or through membership of standing committees.

Street lighting, road maintenance, the provision of fire engines and night policing all fell within the competence of the parish vestry in Dublin, although there was a noticeable change towards the end of the eighteenth century as more and more of the parish functions passed to statutory bodies. Provision for the parish poor was one area however which remained a vestry matter long after 1800. St. Mark's is unusual in that the parish 'poor books', dating from October 1772 survive in near complete, if untidy form. They provide a valuable insight into the charitable functions of the vestry and give some insights into local poverty. The year 1772 was particularly significant in the history of aid for the city's poor. In this year the act of parliament which established *inter alia* the city's House of Industry came into effect, and the new initiative at city level evidently stimulated parish activity, at least in St. Mark's; old measures were, it seems, revived in the new enthusiasm for ending the endemic nuisance of large-scale street begging and vagrancy. The next three decades were a particularly active phase in the involvement of St. Mark's vestry in the welfare of the parish as a whole.

The first extant St. Mark's poor book of 1772 begins by listing the names of sixty-one poor. It can be seen from the outset that the church wardens, the two most senior lay officers in the parish, compiled the records in a thorough manner. Some of those on the schedule of poor householders were struck off the list when circumstances changed; one woman, for example, a widow Hutchinson, was refused relief for having a legacy left to her in England and lending money out on interest.[7]

The poor books account for the various monies the vestry received and their subsequent distribution to the scheduled poor. Poor money was raised by various means. The most important source of income was generated through Church of Ireland church collections at regular Sunday services and, more importantly, those taken at church festivals - Christmas day, Easter Sunday and Whit Sunday. On Sundays there were normally two services and consequently two collections, one in the early morning and one at noon. The size of the collection at these two times varied markedly; for example, on 25 May, 1800 the amount collected at the earlier service came to 3s.8 1/2d. and at midday to £3.17s.9d. If one assumes that the alms-giving members of the congregation donated on average one penny to the plate, then only around forty attended the early services, and over six hundred were present at the midday services. It is unlikely that the total Church of Ireland population approached this figure, so presumably midday collections were swelled by the largesse of wealthier Protestant residents.

Feast days saw a marked rise in the amounts collected. Between 1772 and 1799 the average amount taken on Christmas day was £6. This contrasted with the average Sunday collection for both services which was between one and two pounds. Easter and Whit Sundays also saw heavier alms plates. On Easter Sunday, 12 April, 1789 the very high sum of £7.0s.9d. was donated. Ordination day was another important event in the collection calendar; thus on 24 October 1784, £2.13s.10 1/2d. was received. On these special occasions, congregation size was obviously greater than average, but individual donations were it seems above the norm. The religious importance of alms-giving was traditionally emphasised on the main feast days.

The charity budget could be added to significantly by means of special services, the centrepieces of which would be a 'charity sermon' given by a popular preacher, usually from outside the parish. In St. Mark's these were most often for the benefit of the parish charity schools. But other city charities were allocated a particular date in the year when they could make their appeal. Some such services were advertised weeks in advance in the press. Charity sermons were ostentatious occasions at which attendance was socially obligatory.

Another source of charitable finance for the vestry were direct donations of money, usually as bequests. In June 1774, £20 left by a Mrs. St. George was divided among some twenty residents of the parish who had been recommended as real objects of poverty by three leading parishioners. In January 1788 the church wardens received a legacy from the recently deceased Lord Lieutenant, the Duke of Rutland, to the value of £10. Between 1800 and 1818 regular donations were made by Sackville Hamilton, usually of £5 on Christmas day until his death, when it was recorded that he had left a bequest of £15. The death of wealthier parishioners brought the prospect of such additions to the parish's charitable capital; one of the largest was for £50 left to the parish poor in 1808.

Charitable income was also raised by the collecting of fines, some for breaking corporation by-laws, others for infringing parish regulations. Coal porters, who were ever present on the parish's quays, were regularly fined by the Corporation - probably for fraudulent measures - and the fines were passed on to the parish coffers. Coachmen were also frequently fined; on 30 April, 1802 for example, one coachman had to pay as much as 16s.10d. for reasons unknown. Traders were another target for fines, usually on the grounds that they were dealing on the Sabbath. In some seasons, such as in the spring of 1792 when the Sunday collection rarely exceeded £2, the income from fines overtook all other revenues; one fine alone, that received on 20 April of £8 via the Lord Mayor from colliers, transformed the charitable budget.

Another method of securing funds for poor relief was by charging for tolling the parish bell at funerals. The sum of 2s.81/2d. (a British half-crown) appears regularly throughout the records as being given to the church wardens to pay for the bell being rung in honour of deceased persons. Money was regularly paid to the vestry to purchase flatstones or headstones for graves, a service which seems to have generated considerable profit.

*   *   *

The money collected by these means was distributed primarily to those on the regular 'poor list'. In addition to supporting between forty to ninety 'regulars' in these years, the parish usually reserved some money for the 'sundry poor'. A sense of compassion is reflected through some of these entries; for instance on 8 November, 1784 'to sundry poor objects at the Church door' was paid the sum of 4s.4d.; in November 1804, 1s.1d. was given to a man whose leg was cut and the following March he was given a further 2s.2d.

Money was also given to people in transit so that they would not become a long-term burden on the poor funds of the parish: on 19 July, 1774 a sailor's widow going to England was given 2s.2d.; on 2 November, 1777 Mary McGines 'going to Armagh' was given the same amount.

Money was occasionally distributed to people not on the official list who had been recommended by obviously influential people in the parish; on 5 October, 1771, 2s.2d. went to a dying woman recommended by Mrs Jones; in January 1782, £1.13s.3d. was paid to several poor people 'in fevers' recommended by Dr. Adamson.

Some money was reserved for extra items which helped in the maintenance of the parish relief system, such as in February 1801, when two keys for the vestry money-box were purchased. Bread for distribution was one item which appears in seasons of high food prices; this was however a fairly marginal activity, the purchase of 50 loaves at one point in 1774 being an unusually large initiative. Money was also paid to people who helped the vestry members carry out their duties: on 9 April 1775 one Mrs. Tucker received 5s.5d. for getting change for two years and carrying money to the sick poor, providing bread and 'further trouble'. On two occasions, in 1802 and in 1803, money was spent on paintings as gifts to those who had made donations, as a token of the parish's appreciation. In June 1802 a modest 4s. was paid by the church wardens for a painting which was given to a Mr. Lamb who had previously donated £19.6s.9d.to the vestry in December 1801. In 1803, 3s.10d. was paid for a painting of the social reformer and former Chief Secretary, Col. Blacquiere, who had bequethed £10 towards poor relief in the parish.

Of fundamental importance to the St. Mark's vestry, especially in the twenty years after 1800, was the provision made for selected widows in the parish; a widow's house was consequently established, presumably by bequest. This is first mentioned in the vestry records on 7 November, 1803 when coats were purchased at a cost of 1s.1d. each. On 5 March, 1804, a long list of articles were bought, including coal, ten blankets, ten coverlets, twenty sheets, two hundred yards of linen, thread, sweeping brushes and bellows, which could imply that the house was on the point of being opened. There are numerous subsequent references in the parish records regarding the general maintenance of the house; in August 1813 for example, a group of four carpenters were paid £29.10s.10d. for work completed in the house - presumably in extending it. In September 1814, a Mr. Williams was paid £1 for painting in the house and in May 1816 the house was whitewashed for £1.2s.9d.

The system by which the house was organised appears to have been a strict one, yet motivated by humanitarian instincts. Those within the house seem to have been tolerably well cared for: in January 1803 for example, twenty-seven pairs of women's shoes were bought for £6.11s.71/2d. and there are frequent references in the vestry books to the purchase of shifts and petty-coats. Widows prepared to wash sheets were paid accordingly - in 1804 the comparatively generous sum of 1s.4d. was given to one widow for washing four pairs of sheets. Those who cleaned the clothes and bedclothes of ailing inmates were rewarded; in December 1814 a widow who washed the blankets and sheets belonging to Widow Shepherd, on her entering the fever hospital, was given 9s.11d.

A cook was also hired for the alms house; a Mrs. Hughes was paid 3s.3d. at irregular intervals. On Christmas Day, Easter Sunday and Whit Sunday a special meal was prepared.

The ingredients noted in the records are the same throughout. For example, on Easter Sunday, 1814, two legs and loin of mutton, fourteen loaves of bread, 31/2 stones of potatoes, 21/4 lbs. of butter, plus oatmeal, turnips, cabbage and porter were included. Considering that at this time only fourteen widows were resident in the house, one may conclude that they were adequately fed.

The number of widows in the house did not vary greatly over the years; there were seven widows in the house during the last two months of 1804, together receiving 5s.5d. By July 1819 there were fifteen, receiving 8s. - a much lower per capita allocation. The small number in the house would imply that it was a bequest solely for Church of Ireland widows. At this time a far greater number of poor widows were being catered for outside the alms-house although obviously not as well. In February 1805 for example, the eight widows within the house were given 6s.6d., while thirty-seven widows outside were given 3s.3d.

In general it seems that the poor relief system in St. Mark's parish reflected a degree of bias towards the Protestant poor. This is not always explicit, but we know that of the sixty-two poor receiving out-relief from the vestry in November 1801, forty-one were Protestant and twenty-one Catholic; in March 1804, of the fifty-four poor, thirty-seven were Protestant and seventeen were Catholic. The fact that Catholics were being catered for at all is worth emphasising, given the paucity of funds and the large numbers of impoverished persons who were practising members of the Established Church.

In the early 1770s the regular monthly payment distributed to those on the poor list was 1s.4d. By the late 1770s this had doubled to a British half-crown (2s.81/2d.) and was subsequently raised in 1791 to 3s.3d. In the 1770s about £6 per month had been expended on allocations to those on the poor list and by the early 1790s this amount had risen to between £8 and £10. In 1796 there was a sharp fall to £6 again, reflecting a drop in Sunday collections, but this was rectified as the new century approached. It is difficult to know whether the amount spent on relieving the poor in distress mirrored increased collections, or whether it was a response to a particularly severe time of hardship caused by high food and fuel prices or heightened unemployment. In the short-term, the timing of increased allocations probably reflected the demand for relief, but rising revenues allowed for this flexibility. £50 had been collected in the course of 1773 and by 1792 this had risen to £260. In nominal terms at least, the wealthier parishioners had more to give in the 1790s than in the 1770s. Bad years however, could affect all. The collections, even on special days, could reflect this. Thus in the middle of the appalling winter of 1783-4, the Christmas day collection was only £2.15s.11/2d. In the last quarter of the eighteenth century there was only one lower Christmas day collection - in 1777.

In very bad seasons, the parish came under obvious pressures; 1784 was one such trial and 1800-1 another. During the latter period there was much local distress, due to the very high food prices caused by the harvest failures of 1799 and 1800. From the spring of 1800 to the autumn of 1801, food prices were higher than at any time since the 1740s. Accordingly the number of people regularly receiving relief from the parish vestry rose sharply to about seventy. The amount distributed on a monthly basis increased from around £15 in January 1800 to £55.9s.41/2d. in March 1801, then to £96.8s.0d. by December 1801. However there is no record of any increase in parish expenses in 'poor burials' which implies that although this was a time of great distress, the mortality rate among the poor was controlled by the voluntary action and response of the local alms-giving population.

The vestry books also reveal the distress caused by economic recession and food shortages after the Napoleonic Wars. From 12 January, 1817 to 29 March, 1817, only £53.17s.81/2d. was collected and distributed. The fact that the alms decreased in amount rather than increased - as in the 1800-1801 crisis - reveals that the effects of the depression were more evenly distributed throughout society. Judging by the evidence from other parishes, the death rate in these years probably did rise sharply.

Thus in the late eighteenth century at least, the system of poor relief in the parish of St. Mark's seems to have been adequate, or at least more than nugatory, despite its apparent bias towards the Protestant poor. The numbers catered for were of course small, but this meant that those who were on the list were assured of concrete relief. By the 1790s the parish was losing much of its influence in the administration of local utilities, but it was not yet an obsolete civic institution as its involvement in poor relief amply demonstrates.

NOTES

1. Francis White, *Report and Observations on the State of the Poor of Dublin* (Dublin, 1833), p.9.
2. Rev. James Whitelaw, *Essay on the Population of Dublin....* (Dublin, 1805), p.14.
3. Ibid.
4. Ibid., pp.33-7.
5. Ibid., p.14.
6. Ibid., p.50.
7. St. Mark's Parish Poor-Books, 1772-99; 1800-20: Representative Church Body Library MSS. These volumes are not fully paginated, therefore detailed references for statistics etc. are not given. However these can easily be traced as entries in the poor-books were made in chronological order.

APPENDIX I

Population Density and Waste Houses in St. Mark's, 1798

	Inhabited Houses	Residents per House	'Waste' Houses as % of Total Houses
A. Thoroughfares			
Townsend St.	136	13.1	12.8
Fleet St.(pt.)	40	13.2	7.0
Poolbeg St.	42	12.3	9.1
Moss St.	34	13.8	10.5
Boyne St.	27	15.6	-
Hawkins St.	29	11.3	9.4
College St.	15	13.1	11.8
Gloster St. S.	11	14.5	-
Cumberland St. S.	21	6.0	19.2
Westland Row	4	16.7	-
Leinster St.(pt.)	2	25.0	-
Nassau St.(pt.)	5	5.4	16.7
Grand Canal St.	'no houses as yet'		
TOTAL	366	12.7	10.5
B. Quays			
George's Quay	30	22.6	-
City Quay	41	14.2	-
Sir J. Rogerson's Quay	28	18.5	-
Aston's Quay	17	19.6	5.6
TOTAL	116	18.2	0.9
C. Side Streets, Lanes			
TOTAL	164	11.7	9.9
PARISH TOTAL	646	13.5	8.8

Source: Whitelaw, *Essay*, appendix 'Population Tables: St. Mark's Parish', n.p.

THE CONDITIONS OF DEBTORS AND INSOLVENTS IN EIGHTEENTH CENTURY-DUBLIN

DAVID KELLY

Eighteenth-century Dublin, for all its economic vitality, experienced very sharp short-term changes in its business climate. It was partly because of this that trade depended on the maintenance of extensive and informal networks of credit and debt. Economic success was often a measure of the quality of one's credit network. From the bankers in Castle St. to the tanners in Watling St., all types of trader were inevitably involved in the borrowing or lending of money - and the problems that ensued. Default and insolvency was of course worst in periods of business depression, but even in times of recovery, default was an everyday occurrence: growth encouraged risk-taking in speculative ventures, and traders were tempted to expand their credit relative to their capital base and were thus exposed when economic circumstances changed. For the system of credit to work tolerably smoothly, the legal procedures governing indebtedness had to be shown to be effective.

Under the 1757 legislation which empowered the Recorder of Dublin to hear twice yearly civil bills for sums over £2 and not exceeding £20 in all actions of debt, creditors had first to attempt to levy the sum of the goods and effects of the defendant - where the sum contained in any decree did not exceed £10.[1] If this sum were not paid within three months of the decree, then execution was to be issued 'against the body', i.e. the debtor was to be imprisoned. A debtor could also be placed in gaol while awaiting trial of a suit against him in default of bail where arrest had been made, on the instructions of his creditor. Thus, two kinds of imprisonment for debt were possible: imprisonment on 'mesne process', while awaiting the outcome of the suit and imprisonment on 'final process', where the creditor acted 'in execution' and proceeded against the body of the defendant (strictly an alternative to proceeding against his property). The debtor imprisoned on final process was, in normal circumstances, dependent upon his creditor for his discharge. There was a limitation of six years on actions for recovery of debt in all suits of account

> other than such accompts as concern the trade and merchandise between merchant and merchant, their factors or servants...all actions of debt grounded upon any lending or contract without speciality, all actions for arrearages of rent.[2]

Despite the fact that the recovery of small debts by a variety of means was the subject of Irish legislation, there was no statute which allowed for the recovery of larger sums through process against the debtor's property; the only option was to confine the debtor to prison unless the debt fell within the terms covered by the laws relating to commercial bankruptcy (which are discussed below). The lack of an efficient alternative to imprisonment was seen as encouraging creditors to exercise their discretionary powers to the full. Except in cases of bankruptcy, neither land, nor liquid assets such as bills of exchange, could be seized for payment of debt. No arrangement could be made for taking a part of future earnings in settlement. Thus the confined debtor was seen by society as the victim of a whimsical and inefficient process, but changes in the law were opposed by those who believed that the existing system provided in many cases an effective if unsophisticated mechanism for securing payment of debts. Most suits reached some kind of compromise before the debtor was actually incarcerated.

The long-term imprisonment of debtors was therefore not a necessary consequence of the legal process, but a sign of its periodic failure. An action was not brought against someone who was penniless, per se, or who simply had a balance of debts over assets, but because he had contracted a financial obligation which he failed to discharge. A creditor could try to pressurise or browbeat a debtor into payment and if these attempts failed, the main weapon in his arsenal, the power to threaten imprisonment, might be employed. A court appearance might well concentrate the mind of a debtor into re-ordering his priorities and finally settling the debt. Creditors themselves were often walking a financial tightrope. A letter in *Faulkner's Dublin Journal* referred to the possibility of a creditor suing his debtor and ending up in debtor's prison himself, unable to pay the cost of the action,'and then it is odds but he relieves the defendant as sentinels are relieved by taking the post the other has quitted'.[3]

Mesne process imprisonment, the second form, was not indeterminate and could end when the suit came to trial. It was possible for a debtor, imprisoned on mesne process, to settle with his creditor, terminating the suit before it came to trial.

Creditors cannot have had high expectations of those debtors confined on final process. When debtors held out against their creditors long enough to be imprisoned, the chances of their paying at all - unless compelled - were slim. Committal to prison reduced still further the chance that a debtor would pay, if only because when news spread of his going to prison, his creditors would hurry to slap writs on him. The eighteenth-century proverb that 'a prison pays no debts' encapsulated the feeling that imprisonment for debt represented the failure of the system.

The law could equally be exploited by debtors as well as their creditors. A bailiff's powers of arrest were strictly circumscribed; he could not make an arrest at night and a statute from 1695 prohibited the execution of any writ or process on the Sabbath.[4] Neither could the bailiff break into a house in order to effect an arrest. If he infringed any of these conditions, he was acting *ultra vires* and could be resisted by force. Even when apprehended, a debtor was under no obligation to surrender what he had, unless the creditor attempted to proceed against his property. If instead the creditor chose to proceed against the debtor's body and keep him in prison, the debtor could retain everything he owned and spend it as he pleased.

Because imprisonment actually offered the debtor protection for his property, some men chose to have themselves imprisoned on 'friendly actions', which could be dropped at any time. The preamble to the act, 7 Wm.III, c.25, recorded that

> many persons, out of ill intent to delay their creditors from recovering their just debts, continue prisoners who cannot be proceeded against in such manner as they might be if they were at large

and empowered a creditor to seek a writ of *habeas corpus* to have any prisoner owing him money produced in court to answer the case. Creditors, however, still had a claim on the estate of a debtor who died in prison for recovery of the sum owed.[5]

At irregular intervals during the eighteenth century, Parliament passed debtors' relief acts - which authorised the discharge from prison of such debtors then held as would conform to certain stated conditions. Debtors' prisons always filled up whenever there were rumours of a relief act, although many attempts were made to end collusive incarceration at such times. Relief acts generally applied to those persons who were actually confined within the walls of debtors' prisons by legal committals without fraud or collusion, prior to a stated date. Every mesne process prisoner, with his creditors' approval, also had the option of applying for relief. Sheriffs and gaolers were required to make lists of all prisoners for debt in the kingdom on a certain date.[6]

Notice of a debtor's intention to petition for benefit under a relief act had to be served on his creditor ten to thirty days before the petition was submitted.[7] In addition, from the time of the 1729 relief act, public notices were to be inserted in the *Dublin Gazette,* containing the name, trade, occupation and last place of abode of every prisoner, the name of the prison where he was confined and of his intention to take the benefit of the act,

> so that as well all the said creditors as have not charged the said prisoner or prisoners in custody as those creditors who have

had sufficient notice.[8] However the lists of confined debtors in the *Dublin Gazette* and the schedules of petitioners appended to some relief acts give only very general data on debtors; occupational descriptions are tantalising, but information on the last place of abode of the prisoners is often vague, making the task of identifying Dublin's debtors very difficult; linking debtors' schedules with city trade directories has only revealed the imperfections of the latter.

Full disclosure of the debtor's property was required before discharge (with severe penalties for perjury). An exception was made for wearing apparel, bedding for himself, his wife and family, and the working tools and implements necessary for his occupation, the maximum value of which, £5 or £10, varied from act to act. Anyone who had accepted a trust of any estate, real or personal, belonging to any prisoner discharged by the relief acts and who did not within a specified period disclose in writing the trust and the estate entrusted, was forfeit a sum which varied from act to act, plus double the value of the estate so concealed.[9]

Gaolers were obliged during day-time to admit anyone who wanted to see any prisoner whose name was on the list of debtors seeking relief. Those admitted also had the right to inspect entries concerning such prisoners in the prison books 'together with the name of such person or persons at whose suit or suits, he, she, or they are detained.'[10] Benefit would not be given to any prisoner, who, upon being required by any creditor,

> shall refuse to discover and declare the trade or occupation or last place of abode, of the person or persons, at whose suit, he or she are detained, or being called for, shall refuse to come to the lodge of the prison, where he or she is detained.[11]

The debtor's property, as set out in the schedule made by him, was vested in trustees who disposed of the estate for the benefit of the creditors, the residue, if any, going to the debtor.

Notwithstanding a discharge, all debts due and every judgement and decree obtained against a prisoner, still stood good and were effectual in law to all intents and purposes, not only against the prisoners' estate and chattels at the time of his discharge, but also in the future, with the exception of necessary wearing apparel and tools.[12] It was lawful for any creditor to take out a new execution against his debtor, but only with regard to his property. Once released by an insolvents act, a debtor could not be liable to arrest of his person for the same debt which had precipitated his incarceration.

Relief acts benefited not just those in prison, but the likes of James Duggan, a Dublin tailor, whose case was mentioned in the 1715 relief act: he had been deprived of his liberty since 12 September 1705 'by being so long confined to his house, till 5 September last, or thereabouts' when he was finally arrested and apprehended.[13] In 1727, steps were taken to ease the plight of Sir Hans Hamilton, whose estates were in trusteeship owing to his debts. He had been forced to live in Holland for the previous twenty years 'in an indigent condition'.[14]

*   *   *

Bankruptcy became a distinct category of legal insolvency in the eighteenth century; in this, Irish law followed closely, but not exactly English legal developments. In the major legislation of 1771 (a modification of the English 4 Geo.III, c.33), bankrupts were defined as those exercising

> the trade of merchandise in gross or by retail, seeking their living by buying and selling [and] also scriveners, salesmasters, bankers, brokers and factors

who absconded or otherwise sought to evade payment of their debts, with intent to defraud their creditors.[15] No farmer, grazier or drover of cattle could be deemed a bankrupt, unless he also was a *bona fide* follower of one of the above mentioned occupations.[16] 'Bankrupts' were therefore failed wholesalers, 'insolvents' failed retailers, artisans and the rest of the population who could not answer their creditors.

The Lord Chancellor could, upon every complaint made to him in writing against an alleged bankrupt, appoint a commission of 'such wise, honest and discreet persons,' who had full power to investigate the complaints.[17] Representations could be made to the commissioners by a creditor who was owed at least £100, or two creditors, who, between them, were owed at least £150, or three creditors, who, between them, were owed at least £200, and who had made affidavits before a master of the High Court of Chancery concerning the monies owed to them. If the debts were not real, the bankruptcy not proved, or the commission taken out maliciously, then a bond of £200 was forfeit.

Assignees of the bankrupts' estate were chosen at creditors' meetings, held, in the case of Dublin, at the Tholsel or later at the Royal Exchange. No creditor was permitted to vote if his debt did not amount to £10 or over. A bankrupt had to surrender for examination within forty-two days of notice in writing and public notice in the *Dublin Gazette* that a commission had been issued. Any omission or concealment of any part of the estate to the value of £20, or of account books or writings, with intent to defraud, was deemed a felony. The commissioners were to appoint and convene within the forty-two day period at least three meetings for the purpose of examination and, at the Lord Chancellor's discretion, there could be a fifty-day extension for these. Every bankrupt who had surrendered within the specified time was allowed to inspect his own books, papers and writings, in the presence of the assignees or their appointees. The bankrupt was free from arrest in coming to surrender to the commissioners and from the time of the actual surrender (during the forty-two day period) if not in custody.[18]

This comprehensive Irish bankruptcy act was legally flawed, for the 1777/8 act on bankrupts declared that 'it appears that great frauds have been committed by traders not keeping regular books of account'.[19] No benefit of bankruptcy legislation was now to be available to any bankrupt who failed to produce 'fair account books' of all his dealings, bills, debts and credits and household expenses. It also became obligatory to have an inventory at least once in every two years in such books of all effects, debtors and creditors, specifying profits and losses. The problem of verifiable accounts was still very real; a huge legal log-jam built up after the rash of Dublin commercial and banking failures in 1778, which fresh legislation in the next session tried to tackle.[20] And while the law governing wholesale business collapse was still highly imperfect in the late eighteenth century, at least those who became enmeshed in bankruptcy did not normally face the prospect of prison, unlike the merely insolvent retailer or artisan.

*   *   *

In 1791 a British House of Commons committee found that out of some 12,000 bailable writs issued against insolvent debtors in the city of London and the county of Middlesex in the preceding year, only about 1,200 prison committals had ensued.[21] This is one of the few quantitative indications of how long the path between insolvency and prison actually was. Possibly Dublin creditors may have been more vengeful, or Dublin debtors more penurious than their London counterparts. Certainly the prospect of a sojourn in a Dublin debtor's gaol must have concentrated the mind of even the most obdurate debtor. In the city and county of Dublin there were no less than eight fairly grim, and in several cases, literally deadly prisons where debtors could be held: (i) Newgate, originally in Cornmarket, and then transferred across the river to Little Green; primarily a criminal prison, but debtors were from time to time to be found languishing there; (ii) the Sheriffs' Prison, built in 1794 and separated from the new Newgate by the Sessions House; this prison was built to accommodate those unfortunate enough to have been imprisoned temporarily in the private 'lazarettos' or spunging houses; (iii) the Four Courts Marshalsea in Thomas Street, which was a national debtors' prison, containing mainly prisoners brought there 'by *habeas corpus* from other prisons, or [who] have surrendered themselves into custody in discharge of their bail';[22] (iv) the

Prisons in Eighteenth-century Dublin

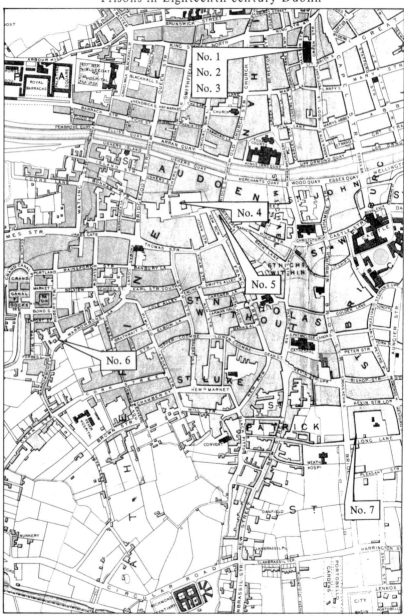

1. Newgate 2. Sheriff's Prison 3. City Marshalsea 4. Four Courts Marshalsea 5. Black Dog 6. Meath Marshalsea 7. Archbishop's Marshalsea.

City Marshalsea, adjoining the Sessions House in Green Street and formerly occupying a site on Merchant's Quay; (v) the Black Dog, which had been an inn in Browne's Castle, Newhall Street; (vi) the Liberty of Thomas Court and Donore (the Earl of Meath's Liberty) which was partly within the city and partly within the county, was served by the Marshalsea in Marrowbone Lane; (vii) the Liberty of St. Sepulchre's (the Archbishop's Liberty), which likewise straddled city and county, was served by the marshalsea in Long Lane, near the site of the Meath Hospital, and (viii) Kilmainham gaol, which served *inter alia* for incarcerating the debtors of county Dublin. The Seneschal of the Deanery of St. Patrick's held no court, so the Liberty of the Deanery, surrounded by the much larger Liberties of Thomas Court and Donore, and of St. Sepulchre, became a sanctury for debtors of small sums. Those taking refuge in it were not amenable to the jurisdiction of the contiguous manors and could not be summoned to the city's Court of Conscience. In 1797 the principal spunging houses where debtors could be initially detained were Benjamin Mathew's in Angel Court, Laurence Mooney's in Angel Alley, Thomas Broomes' in Kennedy's Lane, Thomas Malony's in Church Street; in these 'the conduct of the keepers is in general a scene of unjustifiable extortion.'[23]

What were the conditions in which imprisoned debtors were likely to find themselves? There was a report in *Faulkner's Dublin Journal* on 17 September 1743 that

> the poor debtors in the Four Courts Marshalsea (78 of whom are only subsisted by the charitable allowance of 1d. per day in bread) beg leave to inform the public that they are, with their unhappy families in a most miserable and indigent condition and therefore most humbly request the compassion and charity of all well-disposed Christians.

Such public pleas, not uncommon in the second and third quarter of the century, usually found some response. Moves to remedy the situation the confined debtors found themselves in were undertaken for several reasons. The 1737 relief act noted that many persons, because of the vicissitudes of trade, found themselves in debtor's prisons, and despite their willingness to make what amends they could were still detained there by their

creditors, 'and...such unhappy debtors have always been
deemed the proper objects of public compassion and by several
acts of Parliament have been discharged'.[24] The families of
poor debtors being left destitute was also a cause of public
sympathy. According to the 1729 relief act, many mariners and
other poor people had been committed to various debtors'
prisons in Dublin and

> if they are detained there, their families will become chargeable to the
> parishes to which they belong and in case they are not relieved by this
> act, must perish, no allowance being made by the said prisons to
> support them therein.[25]

The 1749 act set out to ameliorate the condition of

> great numbers of poor people [who] have been and now are
> imprisoned...and have hitherto been deprived of the benefit of the
> several acts passed for the relief of insolvent debtors.[26]

Many poor manufacturers and labouring men often contracted
small debts which they were unable to discharge and
consequently found themselves in the City Marshalsea for
many months,

> without any allowance of food whatsoever and without any possible
> means of earning their own subsistence at the great hazard of their
> healths and even of their lives and to the utter ruin of themselves and
> their families.[27]

Wider anxieties related to emigration and public health. The
1729, 1755 and 1760 relief acts noted the harm being done to
the country's economy by the presence abroad of

> great numbers of workmen skilful in the several trades and
> manufactures, finding themselves unable to satisfy the whole of their
> respective debts and dreading the miseries of gaol, [and who] have
> chosen to leave their employments and native country and have entered
> themselves in foreign service.[28]

It seems likely that many who disappeared to the hazards of the
colonies left debts behind them. Polite eighteenth-century
society had a more immediate fear of

> the deadly infection extending from the precincts of the gaol or crowded
> court-house - [which] with retributive justice visited the homes of the
> wealthy and the houses of the great.[29]

It was generally known that 'malignant fever that is commonly
called the gaol distemper, is found to be owing to want of

cleanliness and fresh air in the several gaols' of the country as a whole.[30] Because many prisons had inadequate facilities for exercising inmates, it was often necessary to take them out onto the streets for that purpose - they were sometimes brought out just to perform their natural bodily functions. There was also the possibility of citizens being infected by prisoners on their way to and from court and even in the court itself. Surgeon George Doyle had been appointed in 1750 to inspect the health of the inmates of Newgate, 'in order to prevent contagious disorders being brought into court'.[31] Testifying to the committee of enquiry into the state of Dublin's gaols in 1767, he stated that by his attendance he had

> caught the gaol fever four different times and was in great peril of his life, three other gentlemen, who attended at one time with him, dying at that time of that disorder.[32]

One remedy proposed was to reduce the number of gaol inmates. Debtors seemed an obvious choice as they were not seen in the same light as common criminals, despite the fact that they often had their wives and children with them in prison. Thus not only were those who should have been in prison endangered, but also a wider circle of associated innocents. Acquitted prisoners, debtors and others could also be detained until they had paid the gaoler's fees (in the eighteenth century common gaolers received no public salary). A debtor, given release from his confinement by his creditor, might still find himself owing money to the keeper or marshal for his fees and rents. If he were unable to pay, he could be held in prison and it was this imposition which spurred the first real reform efforts in the 1760s.

The prime movers behind the bid to clear the prisons of insolvent debtors and of acquitted prisoners were Henry Flood, Sir Hercules Langrishe, Sir John Parnell (the elder) and Henry Sheares. Charles Lucas may also have been involved behind the scenes; he was a frequent contributor to the new opposition paper, the *Freeman's Journal*, which served as a mouthpiece for the prison reformers. The policy of the paper is illustrated by this statement concerning a complaint of malpractice in the Four Courts Marshalsea:

we shall, if not speedily removed, expose [it] to public view: having
on inquiry found some of the facts therein set forth, founded on truth.[33]

The result of the reformers' efforts was that local justices were
empowered to clear the prisons of those held solely for non-
payment of fees, but this law was ineffectual as it meant the
grand juries of counties had to compensate keepers and
marshals for lost fees, which they were reluctant to do.[34] Later
that year, the 3 Geo.III, c.28 (based on English legislation of
1751) attempted to deal with the

many frauds and abuses [which] have been committed by gaolers
exacting exorbitant fees, brewing of drink and baking of bread (which
they oblige their prisoners to take from them at their own rates) and by
keeping their gaols in a filthy and unwholesome manner.[35]

From 1 August 1764 no fee, emolument or gratuity was to be
payable by any gaoler for his appointment. Tables of fees were
to be prominently displayed in prisons and marshalseas. No
brewing by a gaoler or anyone in trust for him, or keeping a
shop for the sale of bread, beer or liquors, was to be permitted.
No cattle were to be kept in the prison yard or houses of
prisoners. The minister or curate of the parish was to distribute
bread to the needy (the distribution of which had in many
instances been taken over by gaolers, to their profit) and the
sexes were to be separated.

Unfair exactions and over-charging continued however, as
did the custom of demanding a 'penny pot' or garnish from
every prisoner. A letter to the *Freeman's Journal* in 1764
detailed the situation in the City Marshalsea where money was
extorted from new arrivals, a practice known as 'brocking'; if
the sum was

not immediately paid by the newcomer, he or she, will be stripped,
naked (and in the case of resistance be pinned fast with cords) carried to
the necessary house and there ducked until almost suffocated and their
cloaths [sic] then pledged until the sum is paid.[36]

The next significant wave of reform was 1778-88, but in the
meantime, attempts to alleviate the suffering continued, with
public as well as private intervention. The Charitable Musical
Society or 'Bullshead' Society, after the tavern in which the
founders met, could trace its origins back to 1723. Concerts

were performed, the proceeds of which helped discharge the liabilities of confined debtors. Membership of the club increased rapidly before mid-century with many noblemen and well-to-do commoners joining. The concerts of the Society were usually performed at the Great Musick Hall in Fishamble Street and the cost of a ticket was half a guinea. The tradition, according to Gilbert was that

> a vast amount of good was effected by this Society, which from its formation to the year 1750, released nearly 1,200 prisoners, whose debts and fees exceeded £9,000, in addition to which a certain sum was presented to each debtor on his liberation. The annual average of prisoners thus relieved amounted to 160.[37]

Private efforts at relief continued every winter season, with events such as the performance in the Theatre Royal, Crow Street, in January 1772 of *The Tragedy of Cato*, 'for the relief of confined debtors in the different Marshalsea' by the young gentlemen of the English Grammer School, Grafton Street'.[38] The receipts for the night amounted to £262.5s.8d. and were applied to procuring the liberation of eighty poor debtors from the Marshalsea.[39] The masquerade at the Musick Hall on the eve of St. Patrick's Day, 1778, attracted a

> Mr. Archdall [who] impersonated the man with the charity box on Essex Bridge (where some debtors from the City Marshalsea were permitted to beg for subsistence) and collected £5.9.10. for the confined debtors.[40]

By this time John Howard was attempting to stir the public conscience at prison conditions in England. In 1775 a group of his admirers in Dublin founded the Howard Society for visiting prisons, but it does not seem to have survived very long. Towards the end of the century there were at least two charitable schemes for debtors: firstly there was the legacy of £800, left by a Mr. Powell, a former debtor, which was administered by the Lord Mayor and aldermen, and from the interest of this a twelve-penny loaf, a piece of beef, some fuel and one guinea in cash, were distributed by the Sheriff on Christmas Eve to each confined debtor in the Sheriffs' prison.[41] Secondly, the Association for Discountenancing Vice (established in 1792 as a charitable education trust with evangelical tendencies) also involved itself with financing the release of small debtors from city gaols. A list of 735 debtors released circa 1799-1801, apparently through the mediation of this body, records the nature of their debts and highlights their humdrum character - rent arrears, debts to hucksters, and debts to money-lenders being the most numerous (see Appendix I). In 1813 the Debtor's Friend Society took over this kind of charitable activity. By its rules, no settlement would normally be made for debts exceeding £5; no debt which was contracted for spirituous liquors would be discharged; and no person who had been found guilty of combination was eligible for relief. The Society's report for the year ending January 1816 stated that seventy persons were liberated from the Four Courts and City Marshalseas and their receipts were £221, including a bequest of £190.17s.1d.[42]

Wider parliamentary agitation over prison conditions had developed in the 1770s and a group had formed around Peter Holmes, M.P. for Banagher and Comptroller of Stamps. It included Sir John Parnell (the younger), later Chancellor of the Exchequer, Sir John Blaquiere, Chief Secretary between 1772 and 1776, and Richard Griffith. Most of these social reformers were close to the Castle, with only Griffith being a firm opposition politician with some radical views. MacDonagh has suggested that this was an example of the Irish House of Commons struggling to develop the limited powers it possessed as compensation for its constitutional weakness. It is striking however that even in 1780 and 1782, the high noon of 'patriot' achievement, prison agitation absorbed a very considerable proportion of parliamentary time.

In 1782, Dublin's prisons were completely cleared of insolvents.[43] A series of investigations into prison conditions followed, with evidence being heard from John Howard and in 1783, from Holmes' friend, Jeremiah Fitzpatrick, who was the only witness not a gaoler, turnkey or magistrate. Holmes' prison act sought to tighten up the 1763 and 1778 acts, enjoining judges on assize to clear the gaols of acquitted prisoners and debtors held for fees only, thereby ending the trafficking with prisoners and preventing 'gaol distemper'.[44]

The prisons act of 1784 dealt with new prison building and the reconstruction of existing prisons while attacking the many reported abuses of keepers and marshals.[45] It had been stimulated by Howard's evidence of conditions in Newgate and in other Dublin gaols. Howard so highly regarded the provisions of this act that it was to be the model for similar English legislation in 1787.[46] Despite Holmes' entreaties in the Commons on 5 March 1784 - 'if ever there was a subject that called more loudly than any other upon the humanity of gentlemen, it is this...' - an attempt to clear the gaols of insolvent debtors failed in the House of Lords.[47] Holmes deplored the rejection of the bill which would have relieved altogether 'one thousand persons whose confinement comprehended the happiness or unhappiness of at least four thousand more'.[48] He hoped another insolvent bill would be taken up in the next session and that

> something be devised, in the meantime, to prevent such a number of persons perishing through want, as no provision had been made by law for their subsistence.[49]

However that bill in turn - which was intended to make creditors provide some maintenance to those for whose confinement they were responsible - also came to naught. A creditor was only responsible for his debtor's maintenance when the debtor petitioned for discharge under a relief act and the creditor required further time to investigate the debtor's assets. The debtor was then detained for an extra period of varying length (the 1715 act specified thirty days) and received a certain allowance as maintenance (the 1729 act allowed 2s.4d. per week).[50] Non-payment of maintenance for a certain time meant discharge for the prisoner.

Fear of gaol fever was revived in the latter part of 1784, and in February 1785 an outbreak in the capital was reported in the newspapers.[51] In July there had been a mass escape from the new Newgate through the sewers and the need for security and dread of contagion seem to have agitated people's minds. It was in this climate that what might be called the prison reformer's handbook was published: Fitzpatrick's *Essay on Gaol Abuses and the Means of Redressing them* appeared too late to influence the 1784 prisons act but nevertheless provided useful ammunition for the reformers.[52] It dealt with the causation of infectious diseases, preventive measures and modes of treatment. Overcrowding, dirt, dampness, foul air, bad or no sanitation, poor food, tainted water, ragged clothes and filthy bedding were condemned as contributory factors in the spread of disease.

In 1786, the office of Inspector General was established, with Fitzpatrick as first incumbent.[53] Dublin was excluded from his remit, but Fitzpatrick undertook an examination of conditions anyway. The insolvents' bill was still before Parliament at the end of May 1786, and with the onset of warmer weather it was feared there would be another outbreak of prison fever. Fitzpatrick reported to the Justices of the King's Bench on conditions he found in the Four Courts' Marshalsea and in doing this he probably speeded up the passage of the debtors' relief act which released one hundred and fifty-six debtors from that prison.[54] In his 1787 report to the House of Commons Fitzpatrick noted that nineteen prisoners occupied thirty apartments while one hundred and fourteen with their families, occupied twenty in the Four Courts' Marshalsea alone. There was a total of one hundred and thirty-four prisoners, thirty-six women, forty-eight children and nine servants, making a grand total of two hundred and twenty-seven. There were thirty-eight beds down and seventy-eight beds up. The prisoners discharged by the recent act exceeded by twenty-two the number of prisoners remaining, and the debts of the discharged prisoners amounted to £22,395.14s.1/2d.[55]

The City Marshalsea was removed from the control of the City Marshal in 1786 and the Corporation was authorised to appoint a keeper.[56] The expose of atrocious conditions in Dublin's gaols in 1787 and the discovery that nobody in Dublin, whether the Corporation, the Lord Mayor, sheriffs or grand jury would accept responsibility for the gaols, led the old reformer Sir John Blaquiere to introduce a resolution placing the onus for inspecting prisons in the capital on Dublin Corporation. This was bitterly resisted, the city opposition being led by Alderman Nathaniel Warren M.P., a Commissioner of Police. An outbreak of gaol fever at the City Marshalsea in June 1787 and the subsequent outcry against Corporation inactivity led to the parliamentary appointment of surgeon John Whiteway as inspector of prisons for Dublin.

With the appointment of an Inspector General for the country as a whole and an albeit ineffectual inspector for Dublin, the campaign for prison reform and debtors' relief was making progress. The relief act of 1785 declared that any prisoner refusing to give an account of his estate and swear to it on oath, was to be treated as a bankrupt although not a trader.[57] The 31 Geo.III, c.21 declared that all prisoners who chose to stay in gaol and 'consume their substance' would be accorded the same treatment. Further debtor's acts followed in 1793, 1794, 1795, 1797 and 1800.[58] The prisons' regulatory act in 1793 entitled the Marshal of the Four Courts' Marshalsea to move from their rooms to the common hall those not paying the rent for their rooms. Persons committed to the prison were to occupy rooms allotted by the Marshal and not to exchange them without his permission.[59] This was to eliminate the practice of prisoners renting out their rooms or part of them to other prisoners, thus depriving the Marshal of his fees. It was hoped that a Marshal who received proper remuneration would have no need to engage in the abuses condemned many times before.

These acts, together with the more strict enforcement of existing legislation, did not necessarily mean that the battle for reform had been won. Progress was slow. Indeed the 1808 parliamentary commission investigating prison conditions found appalling scenes of overcrowding, neglect, inadequate sanitation and squalor on their visits. Only with Warburton and Whitelaw's account of the 1812 visitation can the beginnings of a real change be discerned in the official record, and even this was a curate's egg, with some conditions seemingly little changed.[60]

In the end, what can be said of those who found themselves confined in the various gaols, marshalseas and spunging houses? In May, 1785 Molesworth Greene, a former sub-sheriff of the city, when giving evidence to the committee of

TABLE I

Number of Criminals and Debtors in Irish Prisons, 1759-1800

	Year	Prisoners Tried	Prisoners Convicted	Felons in Custody	Crown Prisoners in Custody	Debtors in Country	Debtors in Dub. City/County	Per Cent of Nat.Tot.
1.	1759	-	-	-	-	705	352	49.92
2.	1765	-	-	-	-	490	228	46.53
3.	1772	-	-	-	-	482	190	39.41
4.	1777-8	-	-	-	-	682	288	42.23
5.	1779-80	-	-	-	-	457	164	35.89
6.	1797	2,672	685	-	-	575	365	63.47
7.	1798	2,991	718	716	1,186	417	199	47.72
	-	-	-	-	-	247	161	65.18
8.	1799	2,470	775	-	1,296	381	208	54.59
9.	1800	2,803	693	-	1,165	488	196	40.16

Sources: (1). Schedule, 33 Geo.II, c.17; (2). Schedule, 5 Geo.III, c.23; (3.) *Dublin Gazette*, 2-4 January 1772; (4.) Schedule 17 & 18 Geo.III, c.14; (5.) Schedule 19 & 20 Geo.III, c.40; (6.) *H. of C. Journals (Irl.)*, XVII, ccxiv; (7.) *H. of C. Journals (Irl.)*, XVII, part 2, dclxxxii-iii; (8.) *H. of C. Journals (Irl.)*, XVIII, cccxlviii-ix; (9.) *H. of C. Journals (Irl.)*, XIX, dcccxlviii-ix.

enquiry, said that in the course of the year he was in office, there were from 1,500 to 1,600 arrests for debt in Dublin, 'which are as many as he apprehends there are in the remainder of the kingdom'.[61] The quality of information on the extent of the problem varies, but some idea of the situation may be gleaned from the figures given in Table I.

Many disparate types of person were to be found in prison, from Abraham Moyers, a Jew and 'notorious cheat' and Henry Thorpe, 'who have severally notoriously imposed on and wilfully defrauded their creditors', to 'the industrious poor, whose labour is cut off with their liberty and who from being useful, become a heavy burthen to society'.[62] Merchants were obviously very vulnerable to imprisonment before the bankruptcy acts, with nine featured on the schedule of 13&14 Geo.III, c.44., along with, eleven grocers, seven vintners, three butchers and five publicans.[63] Others too could be caught in the net; the 1760 legislation for example, relieved John Van Nost, the statuary who made the leaden figure of George II which occupied the niche over the door of the Weavers' Hall in the Coombe, while the 1774 legislation relieved Joseph and Ephraim Thwaites, whose brewing concern continued for many years afterwards.[64] The 34 Geo.III, c.18 limited the time spent in gaol by debtors of small sums and this, together with the procedure followed by the Seneschal of the Liberty of Thomas Court and Donore (which liberty was roundly condemned in the Inspector General's 1797 report for its oppression of debtors), must have helped reduce the number of 'industrious poor' who ended up in prison. The Seneschal in the Meath Liberty heard on his own all cases where the debt was under two pounds, and enquired carefully into the circumstances of the debtor. The debt was allowed to be repaid by instalments, proportional to the debtor's means, imprisonment for small sums being infrequent.[65]

The middle- and upper-middle classes may have gradually benefitted also from a more sophisticated approach on the part of their creditors. The banking system was developing and with it, new means of financing debt were opening up. But the sanction of imprisonment for debt remained in Ireland until

1872, having been abolished in England and Wales three years earlier.[66] Even after that, certain offences still merited punishment by imprisonment, such as non-payment of a penalty other than in respect of a contract, or where a defendant in a suit for debt was about to quit the country. Thus, to all intents and purposes, the Sword of Damocles that had hung over every debtor's head, was finally placed in its scabbard, never again to be unsheathed. The legal distinction between bankruptcy and insolvency was also abolished in Ireland in 1872, the two conditions having long been coterminous in popular usage.[67] This legislation saw the culmination of the efforts of parliamentarians and upper-class philanthropists 'to cheer the face of melancholy in the mansions of despair'.[68]

NOTES

1. 31 Geo.II, c.16 (1767).
2. 10 Chas.I, sect.2, c.6 (1634).
3. *Faulkner's Dublin Journal*, 2-4 Jan. 1749-50.
4. 7 Wm.III, c.17 (1695).
5. 10 Chas.I, sect.3, c.9 (1634).
6. 3 Geo.II, c.20 (1729).
7. 10 Wm.III, c.1; 9 Anne, c.10 (1710); 3 Geo II, c.20 (1729).
8. 3 Geo.III, c.20 (1729).
9. 10 Geo.I, c.11 (1723); 9 Geo II, c.20 (1735).
10. 3 Geo.II, c.20, sect.20 (1729).
11. Ibid., sect.21.
12. Ibid.
13. 2 Geo.I, c.23 (1715).
14. 1 Geo.II, c.25 (1727).
15. 11 & 12 Geo.III, c.8 (1771-2).
16. Ibid., sect.2.
17. Ibid.
18. Ibid., sect. 28.
19. 17 & 18 Geo.III, c.48 (1777-8).
20. 19 & 20 Geo.III, c.25 (1779-80).
21. Joanna Innes, 'The King's Bench Prison in the Later Eighteenth Century' in J. Brewer and J. Styles (eds.), *An Ungovernable People: The English and their Law*...(London, 1980), p.225.

22. 3 Geo.II, c.20, sect.29 (1729).
23. *House of Commons Journals (Irl.)*, XVII, app. p. cciii.
24. 11 Geo.II, c.16 (1737).
25. 3 Geo.II, c.20 (1729).
26. 23 Geo.II, c.17 (1749).
27. 34 Geo.III, c.18 (1794).
28. 3 Geo.II, c.20 (1729); 29 Geo.II, c.16 (1755); 1 Geo.III, c.16 (1760).
29. *Irish Quarterly Journal*, IV (1854).
30. 17 & 18 Geo.III, c.18 (1777-8).
31. *H. of C. Journals (Irl.)*, VIII, app. p. clxx.
32. Ibid.
33. *Freeman's Journal*, 1-2 October 1763.
34. 3 Geo.III, c.5 (1763).
35. British Statute 25 Geo.II, c.36 (1751).
36. *Freeman's Journal*, 29 May-2 June 1764.
37. J.T. Gilbert, *History of the City of Dublin* (Dublin, 1859), I, 76.
38. Ibid., III, 207.
39. Ibid.
40. Ibid., I, 84.
41. J.Warburton, J. Whitelaw and R. Walsh, *History of the city of Dublin* (Dublin, 1818), II, 1053.
42. Ibid., 902.
43. Oliver MacDonagh, *The Inspector General....* (London, 1981), p.146.
44. 21&22 Geo.III, c.42 (1781-2); 3 Geo.III, c.5 and c.28 (1763); 17&18 Geo.III, c.28 (1777-8).
45. 23&24 Geo.III, c.41 (1784).
46. 27 Geo.III, c.11 (1787).
47. *Irish Parliamentary Debates*, II, 415.
48. Ibid., pp.170-1
49. Ibid.
50. 2 Geo.I, c.23 (1715); 3 Geo.II, c.20 (1729).
51. *Freeman's Journal*, 1-3 February 1785.
52. 23&24 Geo.III, c.41 (1784).
53. 26 Geo.III, c.27 (1786).
54. *H. of C.Journals (Irl.)*, XII, app. p. dxxiv. There is no record of the Insolvents Act.
55. Ibid.
56. 26 Geo.III, c.27 (1786).
57. 25 Geo.III, c.46, sect. 26 (1785).

58. 33 Geo.III, c.42 (1793); 34 Geo.III, c.18 (1794); 35 Geo.III, c.30
    (1795); 37 Geo.III, c.49 (1797); 40 Geo.III, c.42 (1800).
59. 33 Geo.III, c.35 (1793).
60. Warburton, *et.al. Dublin*, II, 1053 et. seq.
61. *House of Commons Journals (Irl.)*, XI, app. p. ccccxiii.
62. 4 Anne, c.13 (1705) for Moyers and Thorpe; *Faulkner's Dublin
    Journal*, 2-6 January 1749-50.
63. 1773-4.
64. 1 Geo.III, c.16 (1760); 13 & 14 Geo.III, c.44 (1774).
65. Warburton *et al., Dublin*, II, 1045.
66. 35 & 36 Vict. c.57 (1872); British Acts, 32 & 33 Vict. c.62
    (1869).
67. 35 & 36 Vict. c.58 (1872); British Acts, 32 & 33 Vict. c.71
    (1869).
68. *Dublin Gazette*, 2-4 Jan. 1772.

APPENDIX I

Small Debtors Discharged from Dublin Gaols c. 1799-1801

Nature of Debt	Number	Per Cent
Rent	273	37.1
'Huxtry'	158	21.5
Money/notes borrowed	118	16.0
Legal fees & unrecorded causes	72	9.8
Groceries & other food purchased	41	5.6
Diet & lodging	40	5.4
Cloth/clothing purchased	12	1.6
Miscellaneous goods purchased	11	1.5
Working materials purchased	6	0.8
'Bad money'	5	0.7

Mean size of Debt: £3.16s.0d.
Mean size of Debtors' families: 4.36 persons

Source: Brit. Lib. Add. MS 35,766, Hardwicke papers, ff. 20-42.

NEWGATE PRISON

BERNADETTE DOORLY

Irish gaols in the era before prison reform were crowded, sickly and corrupting places. Conditions in Dublin's Newgate, on the western edge of the old city, were worse than in any other gaol in the country. Gaolers elsewhere extracted money from prisoners for the promise that they would not be transferred to Newgate. In 1728, a six-week stay in the Black Dog prison by John Audovin while he was awaiting execution, cost £300, a large part of which was paid to prevent his being moved to Newgate.[1] Members of the public were also subjected to the threat of the gaol. In the same decade two watchmen were found guilty of extracting money from a former prisoner of the Black Dog by threatening to take him to Newgate. Everyone sentenced by the Judges of the King's Bench, the Lord Mayor or Justices of the Peace for the City of Dublin, was directed to be sent to Newgate. However, only the poorest of them actually arrived, for the constables could be bribed to bring them to more salubrious gaols: 'none are sent to [Newgate]...but those of the poorer sort who are not worth fleecing'.[2]

The management of Newgate typified all that was worst in eighteenth-century public bodies. The position of head gaoler was in the gift of the Corporation and was held by the individual who bid most and who could offer large financial securities. The salary was modest, but the head gaoler was able to charge prisoners for accommodation and for many extras, which in fact made it a highly lucrative position. A parliamentary report of 1729 was the first of many to highlight the abuses within Newgate. It was said to be dirty and neglected, with prisoners receiving neither bread nor bedding, while remaining the captive victims of the gaolers' extortion rackets.

The need for reform was clear but the political will was absent. It was not until the 1760s that an interest in reform originating in England led to any public intervention in the gaol's management. As in England, reform was urged not alone to alleviate prisoners' distress but also to protect the public from the danger of 'gaol fever'. In 1763 the Irish Parliament produced a detailed report on the state of Irish prisons and passed two statutes dealing with prisoners' welfare. The more important act, 3 Geo. III, c.28, established a new system for the supply of bread and provisions to poor prisoners: clergy of the Established Church were to be given funds by the grand juries to buy and deliver bread to those who needed it. Doctors were to be appointed and medicines supplied when necessary.

High food prices in 1766-7 led to an upsurge of vagrancy, and to a public health crisis that affected the city's gaols. A new parliamentary enquiry into gaol conditions in 1767 found that Newgate was then 'in a very ruinous condition'.[3] It was grossly overcrowded: Mr. Doyle, the prisoners' surgeon, estimated that there were 170 prisoners confined in it when 80 was the maximum number it was supposed to accommodate. Fevers were now common - the need for a new prison was explicitly stated. A site on Little Green, on the north side of the river west of Capel St., was provided by the Corporation for the purpose of building a new prison. In October 1773 the foundation stone was laid and the prison completed in 1781 at a cost of £16,000. It was financed by a parliamentary grant of £2,000 but principally by Grand Jury presentments, i.e. by rates on the inhabitants of Dublin.[4] By 1775 these had raised the sum of £4,000, causing, it was claimed, 'great distress' in the city for the poor taxpayers. A city petition to Parliament in 1776 for financial aid to complete the prison met with a favourable response: M.P.s were very conscious of the fact that Dublin had been ravaged that year by a fever epidemic which was believed to have originated in Newgate. Prisoners were moved from 'old' Newgate at the end of Thomas St. in 1780, and the building was

partially demolished; demolition however was halted temporarily
to allow for its use as a prison for prostitutes until 1782.

The new prison was designed by Thomas Cooley, who also
designed the Royal Exchange, now City Hall; it was three
storeys tall with a round tower at each corner and was entirely
built of black calp except for a pediment and centre break of
granite. An apparatus for hanging was situated above the main
door and was used for public executions. This helped to give a
macabre, almost theatrical, air to the prison. Public executions
were indeed great occasions at Little Green. Coffins for the
bodies of those to be executed were sent into the prison a day or
two before the event. The condemned man, who often sold his
body to the surgeons, would celebrate his last night by having a
party with his friends and 'the widow to be', using it was said
his coffin as a table for drinks and cards. The next morning the
hangman would arrive, his face covered by a mask and a
wooden bowl forming a hump on his back to fend off the
missiles with which the crowd invariably assailed him.

It was hoped that the new prison would be secure,
comfortable and would prevent the spread of contagious
diseases. The choice of the site did not favour the fulfilment of
these hopes: Little Green was low-lying, and thus there were
immediate difficulties in the construction of proper drains; it was
an environment that naturally facilitated the spread of disease.
The major problem with the 'new' Newgate however, was
mismanagement. Only a year after the completion of the prison
John Howard, the English reformer, claimed that it was 'the
very reverse of every idea that he can form of a perfect and well
regulated jail'.[5] According to a parliamentary report in 1782, it
was already dirty and crowded, and prisoners were being
crammed into underground cells with men, women and children
sharing the same quarters. There was neither straw nor bedding
and drunkenness was prevalent among the prisoners. It is not
surprising that within a decade there were public calls that
Newgate should be abandoned and a more hygienic and secure
prison be built.

The 'new' Newgate was the recipient of a range of criminal
offenders, from vagrants to those convicted of high treason. In

1798, two of the leading United Irishmen, Oliver Bond and Lord Edward Fitzgerald were held there, both dying within its walls. Newgate also held some debtors, but its main function was as the collection centre for those awaiting transportation from the northern half of the country. The building of the new prison had coincided with a change in transportation policy, for the old destination of the convicts, the American colonies, were no longer available after 1776. Under the acts of 17 & 18 Geo. III, c.9, three to ten years of hard labour on harbour improvements in Dublin port became a substitute for transportation. Many difficulties arose with this scheme in the later stages of the American war and after, not least because Newgate could barely house all those supposedly working in the port. By the end of the 1780s large-scale transportation was revived, with a new destination introduced, Australia.[6]

Newgate offered two types of accommodation: the common hall, which possibly housed the majority of prisoners and the 'private' rooms, for which they had to pay. Those who could afford it paid for the private rooms - often through fear of the common hall where they would be stripped and their clothes sold for alcohol by fellow-prisoners. They would also be at greater risk of infection there, since vagabonds and strolling beggars cluttered the hall. Drunkenness and fighting were common features of the overcrowded life. Deaths from alcoholic poisoning and from wounds inflicted by other prisoners were quite common, even murders were occasionally committed. The common hall did not have windows but slits in the wall through which prisoners suspended alms bags to the street below, the proceeds of which went to pay various necessary expenses such as food and drink. In this way professional beggars could continue to ply their trade from within the prison walls. The hall was heated by a fire in the centre of the room which was 'encircled by desperado's' who excluded the weak and the feeble. A hierarchy existed in the hall, with favoured prisoners often monopolising the meagre space for their own diversions. The men's common hall measured 20 feet by 17 feet.[7] On 18 January 1788 the prison contained 212 prisoners, of which 52 were women.[8] We have no figure for the proportion then living in the common hall but if we assume that a quarter of the men could not afford private accommodation then the number of prisoners sharing the 20 feet by 17 feet was about 40. This would mean that each prisoner had a mere eight square feet of living space. Prisoners in the common hall also had access to a yard which measured 54 feet by 43 feet.

Those in private accommodation fared better although the rooms were by no means luxurious. In 1788 nine pinmakers were living in a two-bed room, each paying 4s.4d. per week for the privilege.[9] No measurement is given for their room; it may however have been the gaoler's apartment or a cell situated on the upper floor of the prison measuring 12 feet by 8 feet, which would have given each pinmaker 10 square feet. These cells lined both sides of the top floor and were divided by a narrow passage where visitors could stand and converse with the prisoners through a grate which opened into each cell.

Men and women were for the most part held in separate areas but 'approvers', those who had turned King's evidence, were accommodated with the women, for which no explanation is given. The parliamentary report of 1782 states that sixteen men were being held in the women's quarters and three women in the men's.[10] Access between the two areas was unrestricted during the day. Venereal disease was common, though not rampant in the gaol. Nonetheless by 1788 it was regarded as a greater health problem than 'gaol fever'. Ventilation was always bad and it deteriorated after 1804 when the prison was surrounded on four sides by other public buildings. The women's courtyard was subject to flooding and the female inmates' lack of exercise was a cause for concern in 1782 when it was described as being 'to the detriment of their health and the possible encouragement of debauchery'.[11] The men's exercise was restricted for fear of escape. By 1792 the gaol was already so dilapidated and overcrowded that the Sergeant's Military Guard was posted there to prevent escapes.

Medical attention was available in the prison although the service was sporadic. Conditions were, however, difficult. In 1788 four women were reportedly in the 'hospital' lying on the ground with no covering, and nothing but water to drink; the hospital area was filthy, and excrement was infrequently removed, which greatly hampered the recovery of the sick. The provision of medical facilities was prompted by two factors, the desire to help the sick and dying prisoners, and the anxiety to prevent gaol fever spreading outside the prison, especially to the nearby courts. The lack of systematic medical care in Newgate, according to the 1782 report, 'endangers the lives of those respectable characters whose duty it is to attend the Courts of Justice as has been fatally evinced in many recent instances'.[12] But the normal conditions of life, at least in the common hall, cancelled out medical provision: the 'deaths of many and the decrepit state of others arise from the want of necessary sustenance, clothing and proper linen'.[13] Although some prisoners were given bread, it was not enough to help those who were too ill to recover, nor to keep healthy those who had to endure such appalling conditions.

The head keeper of the gaol throughout the 1780s was a Mr. Roe, who had inherited the position from his father. He seems by all accounts to have been not alone unable but also unwilling to implement the reforms in Newgate which Parliament sought. He was appointed keeper by the Corporation annually, on the stated condition that he would live in the gaol - which he did not, preferring to let out the gaoler's apartment as private rooms. In fact he visited Newgate infrequently. On his appointment Roe pledged £2,000 security and was paid an annual salary of £120. Of this he paid his assistant £10 per year. He also employed five turnkeys, one of whom was actually a prisoner who received only his diet as wages. The salaries of the others are not recorded.

The position of head keeper seems in fact to have been highly lucrative. Roe, for example, made his money from various sources. Firstly there was the income from rooms let to prisoners: the prison contained at least ten private rooms the prices for which ranged from 9s. to a guinea per person per week.[14] Roe also held the exclusive right to supply the prisoners with various necessities until 1785, when such practices were forbidden, unless under written orders from the Inspector of Prisons or from a doctor. Even after this both Roe and his deputy, Walsh, illegally kept and supplied alcohol in the prison. In order to circumvent the law Walsh later leased out a house opposite the prison. Secondly the gaoler received a fee of 4s.4d. from each prisoner on their release on bail. As it was Walsh's duty to prevent alcohol from reaching the prisoners, it is hardly surprising that 'drunkenness and every species of disorder'[15] prevailed, according to the 1788 report. The provision of liquor to the prisoners was seen by the gaoler and his assistants as necessary to make up for their modest and tardy salaries. No attempt was made by the head gaoler or his assistants to preserve order in the prison. This is hardly surprising since they profited from disorder: the gaoler, by more people being willing to pay high prices for private rooms for fear of the common hall, and his deputy through the continued availability of alcohol in the prison. The various schemes engaged in by other prison officials for monetary gain can only be guessed at.

As far back as 1748, when John Wesley reported in his journal that he preached in the prison but found 'no stirring at all amongst the dry bones', there had been a Church of Ireland chaplain attached to Newgate. The 1763 act had outlined the duties of chaplains attached to gaols such as the buying and delivering of bread to the prisoners in need (which was paid for weekly by the Grand Juries) and also the visiting of inmates. When the prisoners were moved from the old Newgate their chaplain did not accompany them, although a chapel was part of the new building. It was not until 1786 that provision was made for a minister. Following an act of that year a chaplain of the Established Church was appointed to say prayers on Sundays for the Protestant prisoners, to inspect the quality of the prisoners' bread and to ensure that they did not exchange it for what they might consider to be their more pressing needs; the Rev. Gamble took up office in the prison in June 1786 at a salary of £60 per annum. He was also required to visit the prisoners three times a week and 'admonish' those who would not attend prayers.[16] By 1812 the prison had three chaplains, a Dissenter, a member of the Established Church and a Roman Catholic, each with a salary of £100 per annum.[17]

Despite the many enquiries into the state of gaols in Ireland and the recommendations and laws passed to improve conditions in prisons, very little was achieved. It was not until 1794 that some improvement was reported there. The 1788 report had recommended that Roe, his deputy and turnkeys all be dismissed. The new head gaoler, Tresham Gregg, seems to have played a vital role in the subsequent, if short lived, improvement. The prison was reported in 1794 to be clean and well ordered, prisoners were receiving their allowance of bread twice a week, straw and beds were available and the infirmary was well run. Although Gregg was no doubt instrumental in this reform, Sir Jeremiah Fitzpatrick, the Inspector General of Prisons played a key part. His reports to the House of Commons' investigating committees which were the cause of Roe's dismissal and Gregg's appointment also led to the overcoming of Corporation opposition to the appointment of an Inspector for Dublin. In June 1787 Surgeon John Whiteway was named to that post, but he was somewhat ineffectual and lacked Fitzpatrick's commitment.

The annual reports to Parliament on the state of the prison between 1788 and 1792 provide the best profile of eighteenth-century Newgate. The daily average number of prisoners held in those years was 178, ranging from 113 in 1790 to 239 in 1791. The percentage of those awaiting transportation increased from 18 per cent in 1788 to 46 per cent in 1792, a proportion which was stable throughout the 1790s. This may have been due to judges on assize no longer commuting capital sentences to 'hard labour'. The percentage of prisoners confined under Rules of Bail was also decreasing, from 25 per cent in 1788 to 3 per cent in 1792, a drop which may possibly be linked to prison reforms and the change of head keeper in Newgate. The percentage of those not tried also decreased from 48 per cent to 21 per cent.

The 1798 report to Parliament contains the most detailed information on the inmates of Newgate:[18] some 515 persons had been brought to trial from Newgate during 1797 after having been held on remand there. Of these, 152 were sentenced to imprisonment, 86 were transported, 4 were under sentence of death, and two had been executed. On New Year's Day 1798,

TABLE I

Convicted Prisoners in Newgate, 1 Jan. 1798

Sex	Crime	Nos. awaiting transportation (7 years or life)	Nos. serving sentences of 6 months or less	Nos. serving sentences of more than 6 months	Nos. sentenced to death but sentence commuted
FEMALE	Theft	28*	-	2	1
	Vagrancy	10*	-	-	-
	Keeping a bawdy-house	-	-	1	-
MALE	Theft	21*	1	1	3
	Receiving stolen goods	-	-	1	-
	Vagrancy	-	-	-	-
	'Running from reform school'	1*	-	-	-
	Administering illegal oaths	7*	-	-	-
	Forging banknotes; coining; passing bad money	1*	4	-	-
	Conspiracy to murder	-	-	10	-
	Libel	-	-	1	-

* An unknown proportion of those under sentence of transportation had their sentences commuted to indefinite detention in Newgate

Source: *H. of C. Journals (Irl.)*, XVII (1798), app. p.clcxv et seq.

there were 126 prisoners actually confined in the prison, 33 of them on remand and 93 held after sentencing. A breakdown of the latter group shows how important transportation had become by the 1790s. All those convicted of swearing oaths as members of secret societies were sentenced to transportation for life. Prison sentences were generally short, the majority being less than one year and none longer than three years (see Table I).

The improved administrative standards of the early 1790s do not seem to have survived 1798. Ugly rumours circulated the city that the head gaoler was charging relatives for the return of the bodies of the executed rebels.[19] After the Union, parliamentary scrutiny was less close; however a damning report in 1808 found that disorder and mismanagement had returned to Newgate. The sexes were once more mixed, there was no beds or bedding; rape, robberies and murder were occurring and the illicit profits were once again being shared out among the turnkeys and the watchmen. But after the 1810 act of Parliament for correcting abuses and redressing grievances in gaols, the situation in Newgate seems to have swung back towards amelioration. This improvement was attributed to the Chief Secretary William Wellesley-Pole, who repeatedly visited and personally inspected the gaol.[20]

The appalling conditions in Newgate up until then had been caused by the unchallenged position of the head gaoler and the failure of the Dublin Grand Jury to fulfil its legal responsibilities. From 1778 the 17 & 18 Geo.III c.28 had authorised Justices of the Peace to order the refurbishment of local gaols, funded by Grand Jury presentments[21]. 23 & 24 Geo.III, c. 41 decreed that Grand Juries were to nominate from their own members one or more Justices of the Peace to visit gaols and provide the necessary finances, by presentments, fot the purchase of beds, blankets and clean straw. Both these acts were ineffectual. When it came to payment the Grand Juries were invariably slow. Provision for prisoners, such as straw or coal, was bought by the gaolers who should have been reimbursed by the Justices of the Peace. However they often waited up to two years before receiving payment which obviously led to the gaolers neglecting to provide provisions.

The failure of the Dublin Grand Jury to ensure that Newgate was a well ordered and humane penitentiary must be seen as the main cause of the dreadful conditions and its reputation as 'a hot-bed of vice'.[22]

NOTES

1. *H. of C. Journals (Irl.)*, III (1729), app. ccclxxxviii.
2. Ibid.
3. Irish Statutes, Vol. IX (1763-7), chapter xxviii.
4. J. Warburton, J. Whitelaw and R. Walsh, *A History of the City of Dublin* (Dublin, 1818), II, 1047.
5. *H. of C. Journals (Irl.)*, X (1782), dxxiii.
6. *H. of C. Journals (Irl.)*, XII (1788), dxxiv.
7. Warburton et al., *Dublin*, p.104.
8. *H. of C. Journals (Irl.)*, XII (1788), dxliii.
9. *H. of C. Journals (Irl.)*, XII (1788), dcccxxxiv.
10. *H. of C. Journals (Irl.)*, X (1782), dxxxiii
11. *H. of C. Journals (Irl.)*, X (1782), dxxxiv.
12. *H. of C. Journals (Irl.)*, X (1782), dxxxiii.
13. *H. of C. Journals (Irl.)*, XII (1787), dxxiv.
14. *H. of C. Journals (Irl.)*, XI (1785), ccccxiii.
15. *H. of C. Journals (Irl.)*, XII (1788), dccxxxiv.
16. Irish Statutes, XIII (1785-6), chapter xxvii.
17. Warburton et al., *Dublin*, II, 1052.
18. *H. of C. Journals (Irl.)*, XVII (1798), clcxv et. seq.
19. Warburton et al., *Dublin*, II, 1049.
20. Ibid., II, 1048-51.
21. Irish Statutes, XII (1781-84), chapter xil.
22. *H. of C. Journals (Irl.)*, XII (1788), cxxx.

THE SICK
AND INDIGENT
ROOMKEEPERS' SOCIETY

DEIRDRE LINDSAY

In the early part of the nineteenth century Ireland, unlike England or Scotland, was still without any system of public welfare, any general policy to contain poverty. It was not until 1839 that the controversial 'workhouse' poor-law system was introduced. Prior to that, bad harvests and trade depressions had often reduced the perennially poor to utter destitution, with urban centres being particularly subject to recurring periods of malnutrition and disease. The absence of official relief agencies meant that it was left to private individuals and institutions to try to ease the lot of the poor through voluntary work and charitable funding. In Dublin, the scale of metropolitan 'distress', to use the contemporary euphemism, can be seen by the extraordinary number of charitable organisations which were exclusively concerned with the poor of the metropolis. The fact that these organisations were often completely dependent on the generosity of the city's inhabitants reveals something of the charitable ethos of the society: 'few capitals in Europe have in proportion to their population more charitable foundations than Dublin has at present', wrote Warburton and Whitelaw in 1818,[1] and contemporary sources add weight to this claim. The *Dublin Gazette* of July 1822 reported that among the beneficiaries cited in the will of Henry Downing esquire of Dublin City were the Female Orphan House, Circular Road; the Old Man's Asylum, Russell Place; the Strangers' Friend

Society; the Seminary for the Instruction of Deaf and Dumb Children; the Mendicity Institution; and four different hospitals.[2]

It has been claimed that the proliferation of these philanthropic institutions in Ireland was part of the general European trend towards a more humanitarian response to the wretched condition of the poor and also, that it was associated with the evangelical revival in Ireland.[3] The truth of these claims can only be tested through an investigation of individual charities. The Sick and Indigent Roomkeepers' Society was one of the most successful and certainly the most enduring of the charities founded in this period. The history of its origins and development, while in many ways unusual, gives some general insights into the phenomenon of pre-Victorian Irish charities.

The origins and early history of the Sick and Indigent Roomkeepers' Society has been well-recorded despite the absence of the Society's early archives. Warburton and Whitelaw stated that

> a few individuals in the middle ranks of life, inhabiting a part of the town where the population was poor and crowded, had daily opportunities of knowing that many poor creatures who were unable to dig and ashamed to beg expired of want and were often found dead in the sequestered garrets and cellars to which they had silently returned; they resolved therefore to form a society for the purpose of searching out those solitary objects. [4]

The 'part of town' referred to was the area of Charles Street (West) behind Ormond Quay and, although sources differ regarding the individuals involved, all include the following six men among the names of the Society's founders: Samuel Rosborough, wholesale linen draper, 24 Charles Street (West); Patrick Magin, grocer, 14 Charles Street (West); Timothy Nowlan, pawnbroker, 14 Greek Street; Philip Shea, carpenter, 64 Little Mary Street; Peter Fleming, fruitman, 5 Mountrath Street; and Laurence Toole, schoolmaster, Mary's Lane (the latter being appointed first secretary of the Society).[5] These men, and possibly others, met in Mountrath Street on 15 March 1790 and resolved that

> as a charitable feeling for the relief of our fellow creatures must be pleasing to Almighty God we...have resolved unanimously to form a Society, to be called the Charitable Society for the Relief of Sick and

Indigent Roomkeepers of all Religious Persuasions in the City of
Dublin.

A subscription was set - a minimum of 2d. per week or 8s.8d.
per annum. Members would be entitled to recommend 'known
and deserving persons' to be given relief by the Society. It was
laid down that the objects of relief

> shall be poor roomkeepers who never begged abroad and who by
> unforeseen misfortune, sickness, death of friends, or other dispensations
> of Providence, have been reduced to indigence,and that such persons
> must be of good character, for sobriety and general good conduct.

It was also stated as a general principle that 'no political or
religious subjects shall be introduced or allowed to be discussed
at any of the meetings of the Society'.[6]

For its first three years the Society confined its activities to
the poorer households in the Charles Street, Mountrath Street
and Ormond market area, and gave relief in the form of
potatoes, meal, bread, straw, fuel or money, as the
circumstances of the roomkeeper dictated.[7] In 1790, the Society
received £20.2s.4 1/2d. in contributions, and spent £17.9s.8 1/2d.
in the relief of 129 families (516 persons altogether).[8] However,
according to Warburton and Whitelaw's account a quarter
century later, 'the obvious utility of the charity soon attracted
public notice and support', and in the course of 1793 the
Society had received £300.14s.11d. which enabled them to give
relief to 2,957 families (7,785 persons).[9] The need for relief of
the kind which the Society offered was apparent in its rapid
expansion (see Figure I). In 1793 it became necessary to
establish separate meeting places in different parts of the city so
that relief could be distributed more efficiently. Four districts
were set up: in the north-west, the Barracks division; in the
north-east, the Rotunda division; in the south-west, the
Workhouse division; and in the south-east, the St. Stephen's
Green division.[10] The line of Bride Street, Werburgh Street and
Fishamble Street separated the Stephen's Green from the
Workhouse division south of the Liffey, while Capel Street and
Bolton Street divided the Rotunda from the Barrack division.[11]

Each district had a president and, after 1799, a committee of
trustees who were residents of the area; they were to be

responsible for receiving the relief petitions of persons recommended by subscribers at weekly divisional meetings. Each petition presented was investigated by an inspector before relief was given; he reported back to a subsequent divisional meeting regarding the merits of the petitioner. Cases where the petitioner was sick were treated differently and immediate assistance was given to the roomkeepers and their dependants. The records of the Society show a preoccupation with the importance of verifying each claim by inspection; this reflects both the intensity of public scrutiny of the Society's affairs and the genuine problems with which those who undertook the running of a benevolent society had to deal. For similar reasons the Society was scrupulous in its keeping of accounts and regularly invited anyone who so wished to inspect the account books, an offer which was often taken up.[12]

The distribution of relief was normally carried out by the divisional officers. Decisions relating to fund-raising (including the collection of subscriptions) were made centrally at general meetings, which were open to all members and held monthly. Apart from the secretary and treasurer, the executive officers consisted of one and then, after 1797, a second collector, elected by the general meeting to collect subscriptions on a regular basis.[13] They delivered their collections to the treasurer, who also received donations and all other payments. The treasurer then distributed the sums voted by the general meeting to each division according to its needs and the funds available. As the scope of the Society was extended, the numbers of subscribers and of those seeking relief grew. On 10 March 1797, it was decided that a central committee of twenty-one trustees be elected to audit accounts; it would also prepare for and conduct charity sermons, arrange the general business of the Society preparatory to the monthly and annual general meetings, and propose such measures as they might think beneficial to the interests of the Society at large.[14]

In the years after 1797 the committee of trustees seems to have played a dynamic role in raising funds and in increasing efficiency through their constant supervision of the workings of the Society. Its membership consisted of two groups, those

actively involved in the Society's practical business such as
Rosborough, Peter Brophy, Archibald Hamilton, and the Rev.
Joseph Stopford, and secondly, those who were largely
peripheral to it, for example several Fellows of Trinity College
who were elected to the first committee (including the Rev.
John Usher and Dr. Whitley Stokes); their main contribution
was probably to bring prestige to the Society, thereby assisting
indirectly in the raising of funds.[15] Some of the guardians
elected in the early days were anything but conscientious. It was
recorded in April 1800 that there were three trustees who had
not attended any meetings since their election; a resolution was
passed requesting them either to attend or to resign so that
others could take their places, 'as the interests of the Charity
suffer most materially from the non-attendance of the trustees
who were appointed its Guardians' [underlined in MS].[16] The
meetings of the trustees were separate and distinct from the
general monthly meetings until 1810, at which point the two
were amalgamated.[17] This seems to indicate that trustees'
meetings were normally attended by only those who were active
in the Society at large, thus making separate meetings
superfluous.

The need remained, however, for a committee specifically to
deal with fund-raising and with the legal difficulties of gaining
possession of sums donated by bequest. It was the latter
problem, involving in certain cases years of Byzantine
technicalities, which prompted the resolution at the general
meeting of 2 November 1827

> that several sums of money and property have been willed to this
> institution, and for want of an efficient finance committee these sums
> have not been properly looked after and are...totally lost to the
> institution.

A finance committee of twelve men, all active members of the
Society was therefore appointed.[18] From 1828 the number of
Honorary Trustees, 'distinguished for their respectability and
active attention to the interests of the Institution',[19] began to
grow from five to include various wealthy and prestigious
patrons, including the Lord Mayor and High Sheriffs of the

city, the Lord Chancellor, the Provost of Trinity College, and leading clergymen of Dublin, both Anglican and Catholic.[20]

The task of ensuring a constant and adequate level of funding sufficient for the charity to function was always difficult in view of the range and number of charitable institutions in Dublin, each appealing for the special consideration of the public. Among the institutions listed in the report of the Poor Enquiry in 1836 as sharing the Roomkeepers' object of relieving the poor by 'small donations of money, food, clothing and other necessities', were the Strangers' Friend Society, the Benevolent Strangers' Friend Society, the Industrious Poor Society and the Charitable Association.[21] The Roomkeepers' Society relied primarily upon regular subscriptions and upon the less regular but generally more substantial donations from the affluent benefactors to whom the Society made frequent appeals. In this respect, the patronage of the Lord Lieutenant, as the leader of fashion in Dublin Society, was particularly sought after. Lord Cornwallis was the first Lord Lieutenant to donate money to the Society's funds, giving £100 in May 1801. His successor, the Earl of Hardwicke, followed this example with a similar donation in April 1806, commenting that he had 'always considered it one of the most useful charities in Dublin', and paying tribute specifically to the work done by Samuel Rosborough.[22] Donations, frequently in the form of bequests,[23] were in many years the single largest source of income for the Society, but they tended to fluctuate greatly according to the general economic situation and the visible need for relief of the poor: in 1799 for example the level of donations reached its highest since the Society's foundation, totalling £1409.9s.61/2d. - in response to the critical situation in the city. Yet donations during the more prosperous year of 1804 totalled a mere £304.17s.71/2d. The level of income derived from subscriptions in the same period (1799-1804) remained fairly stable, averaging around £580 per year.[24]

The other major source of funding came from charity sermons, 'the great prop of the philanthropist' during the Georgian period.[25] The Society endeavoured to arrange sermons for this purpose in the places of worship of the main religious denominations in the city. The first sermon on behalf of the Society was preached in the Catholic chapel in Liffey Street in 1792, which produced £58.12s.81/2d., and the following year a charity sermon on behalf of the Roomkeepers was preached in a Dissenters' meeting house; there donations totaled £107.18s.8d.[26] Considerable organisation was involved in obtaining a suitable church, the services of a clergyman whose eloquence would have the desired effect, and the attendance of a distinguished, or at least a wealthy, congregation. Again the patronage of successive viceroys was important at the Anglican sermons, while the Catholic sermons were generally supplemented by church collections at Masses throughout the city on the Sunday set aside for the Roomkeepers' Society. The effort expended in running these events was repaid in the boost they gave to the funds. In 1823, the Society's annual report explained the importance of the sermons then being held bi-annually, one in the Established Church at the end of April or beginning of May, the other in a Catholic chapel at the beginning of December. In the interval from May to December, the report stated

> very few donations are made to the funds in consequence of the distinguished characters and other respectable persons being out of the city in the summer season. The sum collected at the sermon in December together with the subscriptions which fall due on the first of January is the only supply for the relief of the poor during the inclement season of winter and until the charity sermon in April or May.[27]

There were several other occasional sources of revenue. Plays were held from time to time for the benefit of the Society - the first such performance in 1794 raised £236.11d.0d.[28] In April 1804, a charity ball was held at the Rotunda, which added £184.12s.6d. to the Roomkeepers' funds; thereafter the 'Roomkeepers' Ball' became an annual event patronised by Dublin's social elite - in 1830 the patronesses included the Duchess of Leinster, the Marchioness of Downshire, the Marchioness of Ormond, the Countess of Meath and the Countess of Annesley. It had as its main object, however, the employment of Irish manufacturers, and patrons were expected

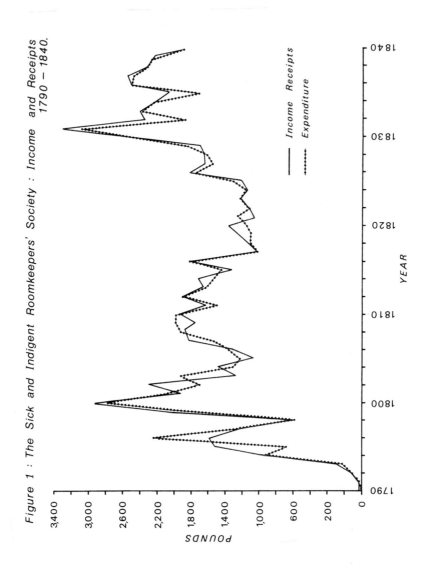

Figure 1 : The Sick and Indigent Roomkeepers' Society : Income and Receipts 1790 – 1840.

to appear in Irish-made garments.[29] Here was a clear recognition of the increased burden which fell on the Roomkeepers' Society in the years of sharp decline of industrial employment. During these crisis periods, the Society was forced to make special appeals to the public, and no one was exempt from its requests: in 1830 the secretary applied to the six Dublin M.P.s for help 'in consequence of the prevailing distress',[30] and in 1837 because of the 'great destitution still existing' the Society sent a delegation to London 'to represent to the nobility and gentry this very great distress' (a venture which only raised £272.4s.0d.).[31]

The records of the Society testify to the imagination, innovation and flexibility with which the members responded to the perennial problem of maintaining the flow of revenue. In 1799, when the disturbed political situation in the city prevented the holding of charity sermons, the Society was forced to make a desperate appeal in the newspapers. They were called on

> to implore your *immediate* assistance - their funds are exhausted and unless a providential supply enables them to continue their usual support, they must in one *week* abandon the numerous objects of their present care.[32]

Again in 1832, during the cholera epidemic, the Society was obliged to vote all the money in hand that month for the relief of distress.[33] A survey of the Society's accounts for the period 1790-1840 shows how closely the receipts and expenditure correspond (see Figure 1).[34] Funds were almost entirely expended in direct relief to the poor. Of the activists and officers of the Society only the secretary received a salary; his was certainly the most laborious and time-consuming office. At the end of 1800 the then secretary, Laurence Toole, received £4.3s.4d. as his salary for one month;[35] in 1817 there was a recommendation that the salary for the new secretary should not exceed £1 per week.[36] In 1828 a second secretary was appointed to assist in the clerical work.[37] The only other members of the Society to receive emoluments were the two subscription collectors who were each allowed six per cent commission. [38]

The Roomkeepers' Society distributed its funds through the four divisional committees, in accordance with the number of petitions from each division. For this reason a larger proportion of the funds usually went to the Workhouse division. For example, the monthly allocation in February 1801 was as follows: Workhouse division 25, guineas; Barrack division 20, guineas; St. Stephen's Green division 20, guineas; Rotunda division 15, guineas.[39] This did not however mean that individuals seeking relief in the Workhouse division received a larger sum *per capita* than petitioners in the rest of the city. In fact, the reverse seems to have been the case; a representative of the Society explained to the Poor Law Commissioners in 1836 that 'the great mass of the poor and weavers live in that division', so that the committee 'divide their money into smaller sums to relieve the greater number'.[40]

The Rev. Thomas Shore, Church of Ireland curate of Saint Michan's and secretary of the society in 1836, identified three classes among the poor in Dublin for the Poor Law Commissioners: those who were 'near-destitute' (of whom he estimated there were 25,000-26,000); those with 'only occasional employment' (25,000-26,000); and those with occasional distress, that is, 'mainly poor tradesmen who would not get a job in a shop and are below the rank of journeymen' (16,000-18,000). The latter groups, he claimed, along with persons in temporary distress due to sickness, would be the usual heads of household who applied to the Sick and Indigent Roomkeepers' Society.[41] The Society made it a general rule that

> single objects, unless in distress, ought not to be considered as entitled to relief as long as the applications of people with families are unattended to.[42]

The *sick* poor were always regarded by the Society as those most deserving relief: they were presumed to have been formerly industrious, honest and 'ashamed to beg'.[43] One of the first steps taken by the Society in this area was to secure the services of several physicians who visited the poor on a voluntary basis in their homes.[44] Later the Society paid an annual subscription to the Dublin General Dispensary, where medicine and advice were given free to the poor 'to enable the [divisional] presidents to recommend sick objects for medical aid'.[45]

The need to combat the spread of contagious diseases influenced the form of relief given by the Society; during the expensive and sickly months of winter it was felt necessary to give the poor extra relief in kind rather than just extra cash. The *Dublin Journal* reported in January 1798 that as well as £100.2s.9d. 'distributed in money and bread', a further sum of thirty guineas was spent on blankets, coals and potatoes.[46] In 1801 Rosborough managed to get Lord Hardwicke's permission for the issue of a thousand pairs of used military blankets for 'sick and indigent Roomkeepers'. (Because of the filthy and infectious condition of the blankets, they had to be 'putrefied and stoved' before they could be handed out.) This was the first of several successful applications to the Commissariat Stores by the Society. They also obtained quantities of cast-iron camp kettles and other canteen equipment for distribution to the poor of the city.[47] It was, in fact, quite appropriate that the government's military stores should be a source of some benefit to the Society, however limited, since many of the petitions arose directly from the continuing drain of city manpower to the army during the first twenty-five years of the Society's existence. During a charity sermon in January 1796, the Rev. Richard Graves informed the Protestant congregation in Saint Werburgh's church that he had been

> instructed to assure you that far the majority of the petitions presented to this society for aid state that the helpless supplicants are reduced to the extremity of wretchedness by the absence of the father, the husband, the son, the brother in their country's service.

This was not just an oratorical technique employed to open the purses of a well-to-do congregation since Whitley Stokes, the physician, philanthropist and erstwhile radical, made the same point three years later. He reported that the Roomkeepers' Society believed that five-eighths of their petitioners were then in hardship due to the absence of the male breadwinner on military service.[48]

The Society was wary of fostering dependency among the poor to whom they were giving assistance. In order to discourage long-term reliance on their relief, a petitioner could only make a second application for relief after four months had passed, although exception was made in the case of sick persons. And although there was always the danger that the charity would be abused, it was repeatedly stated in the evidence given by the Society to the Poor Enquiry that a large section of the poor were reluctant to accept charity unless forced to it by absolute necessity. Several instances were quoted on that occasion of petitioners who, having applied for relief and then obtained work, declined to accept relief subsequently offered, for in the words of John Murray, president of the Workhouse division, 'labour is what they want not charity; they are naturally independent'.[49]

One of the Society's primary roles was in fact the financial nursing of 'tradesmen' through periods of unemployment. The annual reports of 1826 and 1829 specifically blamed the 'general stagnation in trade' and the resulting 'want of employment' in the woollen, cotton and silk trades in the Liberties as the major cause of the sharp jump in numbers seeking relief.[50] In its early years the Society had run an experimental employment scheme: a large house had been rented in Mary's Lane and with three hundred spinning wheels obtained from the Linen Board, a 'School of Industry' was set up, apparently for unemployed adults. The project, successful in the short term, proved too expensive for the Society and was abandoned after a short period; the equipment was then distributed to suitable persons who might thereby become self-employed at home.[51] After this the Society confined itself to smaller-scale projects, such as assigning to 'industrious persons (particularly females) small sums with which to trade, hawk small wares such as delf, glass, fruit, vegetables, fish', or to redeem from pawn their 'implements of trade'.[52] The effect of these schemes in enabling the poor to earn a livelihood again 'without being further burdensome to the Society' was the yardstick by which the Society gauged its own success, and the members of the Society recorded their satisfaction that some of those relieved 'so thrive that they become not only subscribers but active members of the Society'.[53] It was less heartening, and an indication of how the sharp fluctuations in the wider economy affected the individual, that former subscribers and even active members of the Society were sometimes driven to seek relief from the charity. A notable example of this, cited in Charles Sharpe's submission to the Poor Enquiry, was of a man relieved in the St. Stephen's Green division who

> had been a president in the Rotunda division and who, at one time, was considered to be extremely wealthy, and the owner of a first-rate grocery establishment in Britain Street.[54]

Such evidence of the vagaries of fortune among Dublin's population raises the question of the social make-up of the Society. There was clearly a wide range of social classes represented among its subscribers, from foreign royalty such as His Imperial Highness the Grand Duke Michael of Russia, who subscribed £10 in 1818,[55] to the modest tradesmen who subscribed the minimum of 2d. per week. Lists of subscribers for the early period have not survived and before 1823 they exist only in a hopelessly unsystematic form.[56] *Watson's Almanack* of 1797 says that the Society had 'upwards of 2,500 subscribers';[57] if this is correct and given what we know of the Society's total income from subscriptions at the time,[58] these 2,500 subscriptions must have been small and irregular, the vast majority coming from lower-income groups. A profile of the subscribers can be more accurately gauged from the lists contained in the printed annual reports beginning with that of 1823. In that year subscribers' names were divided into two groups: those subscribing the minimum amount required for membership (8s.8d. per annum) - of whom there were 490 persons; and those who subscribed above the required amount (the sums listed are generally from 10s. to £2) - of these there were 213 persons. Thus at that period the Society's membership was dominated by those who paid the minimum subscription. Over the next 15 years, the Society's total membership expanded to more than 900, and the minimum subscribers became an even larger majority.[59] This is confirmed by the testimony of active members who characterised the subscribers as being nearly all 'middle class'; when the 'higher class' contributed to the Society, they nearly always did so by single donations. The Poor Enquiry commissioners in 1836 were led to conclude that of the contributions towards the Roomkeeper's fund

> it appears not merely that the majority in number are contributors of small sums, but that upwards of one half of the whole amount of annual subscriptions is raised in payments not exceeding 10s.6d.[60]

What then of the active members of the Society? We have seen that the founders were mainly manufacturers and retail traders, men engaged in small business enterprises. Among the first divisional presidents were a linen draper, a distiller, an auctioneer, and a paper-stainer/house painter.[61] George Binns, the treasurer in 1796/7 was an ironmonger in Dame Street, and was also prominent in the Guild of Smiths. The man who succeeded Toole as secretary in 1817 was John Grehan, a carver and gilder in North Anne Street. Of the four divisional presidents in 1800, two were woollen drapers, one a cabinet-maker, and one a tobacconist.[62] The involvement of women in the early years of the Society seems to have been limited to the activities of various upper-class 'ladies of the city' who recommended petitions for examination by the inspectors,[63] for although the Society accepted subscriptions and donations from women, its officers were exclusively male and the role of women remained an informal one. The early evidence points towards a Society firmly based on the male tradesmen of Dublin.

At the end of the 1830s the profile of active membership was remarkably similar, except that there were relatively more retail traders involved. Of the four divisional presidents in 1839 there were two grocers; one grocer/wine and spirit merchant; and one carpet manufacturer.[64] The main representatives of the 'higher classes' were by then drawn from the professions; there were numerous clergymen, several medical doctors and a few lawyers who also involved themselves actively in the work of the charity.

If confirmation were needed that the Society was made up and administered chiefly by persons of modest circumstances, additional information can be found in the public debate which began in the 1830s on the question of temperance: until 1855,

when the Society took possession of their present house,
number 2 Palace Street, for use as a central office and a venue
for general meetings,[65] weekly meetings were always held in
public houses; in the eighteenth and early nineteenth centuries
these were the most convenient venues for public meetings and
were available gratis - each Society member paid for his own
refreshments.[66] The custom was however queried by the Poor
Enquiry Commissioners in 1836; one of the divisional
presidents, T.J. Delahunt, a carpenter and builder of Beresford
Street and president of the Barrack division, denied that the
practice reflected badly on the Society. He doubted whether the
'higher orders' would be induced to attend were the meetings to
be held in private rooms, indeed he felt it might discourage the
'humble class' who are

> induced to attend and take the trouble of the institution...I never knew
> any of the higher orders attend our weekly meetings except two
> Protestant clergymen and some Catholic clergy attend sometimes.

The commissioners concluded that the meetings of members
'are almost all made by tradesmen and others dependent upon
their daily exertions for their livelihood'.[67]

A striking feature of the records of the Society is the absence
of any signs of real co-operation between the Roomkeepers and
the other charitable organisations in the city. Formal contact,
when it was made, was generally concerned with the most
effective way of obtaining possession of a joint bequest.[68]
However in times of crisis, such as in 1831, the Roomkeepers
contacted other major charities to prevent undue pressure on
their own funds.[69] Occasionally there was some attempt at co-
operation in fund-raising, such as in August 1831 when a
'Grand Musical Festival' was held for the benefit of both the
Roomkeepers and the Mendicity Institutute, but this met with
little success.[70] John Grehan, speaking with over thirty years'
experience of active work in the Roomkeepers' Society,
commented in 1836 that 'a co-operation with the other societies
might be beneficial, but would be very troublesome'.[71] The lack
of co-operation was perhaps due to nothing more than
administrative convenience. Significantly, the most consistent
example of co-operation was in the arrangement of charity-

sermon schedules so that no two of them would clash to the mutual disadvantage of the charities concerned.[72]

It is obvious that by the 1820s and 1830s, the numerous charitable societies and institutions had far more applications for relief than could be met, such was now the intensity of the problem of urban poverty. The distinguishing feature of the Roomkeepers (of which they constantly reminded the public) was the universality of their provision:

> the truly benevolent, the truly Christian spirit which animated the founders of this Society, as it would not permit them to confine their exertions from private and local attachment, so neither would it permit them to shackle their benevolence by the narrow restraints of religious distinctions.[73]

Warburton and Whitelaw commented on this 'remarkable' feature of eliminating religious distinction not only in its objects, but also in its membership as a 'holy bond of charity' in much the same terms as were used by the Roomkeepers themselves to expand the principle.[74] Samuel Rosborough claimed that equal attention was paid to clerical recommendations, whatever their religious persuasion, with the 'happiest consequence, in maintaining a familiar intercourse between the clergy and the laity of every religious denomination'.[75] The only apparent inter-denominational rivalry was of a positive variety,

> ecclesiasts of all communions coming forward, not to irritate themselves or their flocks by acrimonious controversy, but to rouse them to contend which should most excel in deeds of brotherly love.[76]

It was not always easy for the Society to foster this kind of religious harmony, given the sectarian nature of the community in which it operated. In the 1790s any organisation based on the close co-operation of different religious persuasions was politically suspect in the eyes of a paranoid Dublin Castle. In 1798 the Society's minute books were actually seized shortly before the rebellion. The Society before this had been known as the *United Charitable Society for the Relief of Sick and Indigent Roomkeepers (of all religious persuasions) in the city of Dublin*, but thereafter the word 'United' was prudently dropped from its title.[77] The 1830s were also a period of acute religious tension within the city which touched the Society. There were repeated accusations that petitioners were being questioned about their religion, and that Protestants were being refused relief. The Society normally dealt with such complaints through the appointment of a special committee of subscribers, consisting equally of Protestants and Catholics, to investigate the accusations. These were nearly always proved to be groundless.[78]

A need to demonstrate the Society's multi-denominational character was occasionally necessary - thus the creation of two honorary secretaryships in 1835, one appointee being an Anglican clergyman, the Rev. Thomas Shore, and the other Father John Spratt, a Catholic.[79] But religious animosity continued to impinge on the Society's normal business: in 1836 Shore reported to a meeting of the Society that one member, George Browne, had told the inaugural meeting of a Society for the Relief of Poor Protestants 'that he had quit the Roomkeepers as it was altogether in the hands of the papists'.[80] There is no evidence that Browne's reported allegation was based on fact, and it is possible that personal animosities were vented through sectarianism. In any case, the Roomkeepers maintained their non-sectarian principle to the extent that any inspector who interfered with or noticed the religious belief of any applicant and on that basis withheld a just measure of relief was excluded from the Society and prevented from ever becoming a member again.[81]

A corollary of the principle which forbade any distinction between religious denominations was the the exclusion of any political discussion at the Society's meetings. Moreover, the Society took care not to accept contributions to their funds from any source which might compromise their position as a non-political society, and this was seen by their refusal in 1836 to accept the proceeds of a play staged by the New Histrionic Society.[82] But the following year, the Society felt it necessary to discuss the question of the poor law, since its introduction would obviously affect the operations of the Society. This move in itself was controversial. It was feared that the political differences which had emerged in the course of public debate on

TABLE I

Level of Income from Subscriptions and Donations, 1795-1804

Year	Total Subscriptions			Total Donations		
	£.	s.	d.	£	s.	d.
1795	301	18	61/2	963	1	91/2
1796	383	7	91/2	873	1	6
1797	519	2	11	395	7	51/2
1798	515	8	81/2	321	2	9
1799	415	4	71/2	1406	9	61/2
1800	693	12	10	1380	17	6
1801	610	18	101/2	751	15	11/2
1802	518	13	7	737	11	8
1803	437	19	71/2	547	16	4
1804	528	16	7	340	17	71/2

Source: SIRS, 1028/4/2.

the measure would distract the members from their primary concern which was charity. It was however decided that the question held such serious consequences for the Society's future that it merited discussion. A special general meeting in 1837 expressed 'anxiety' concerning the effect that the levy of the poor rates would have on contributions to the Society's funds. However a resolution was passed which stated their intention to adopt their activities so as to give relief to 'destitute persons who are not fit persons for a workhouse'. It was hoped that the Society would as a result of the new legislation be able to revert to the original purpose for which it was founded,

> a resource for those who would not allow their wants to meet the public eye, but would sooner die in their privacy than seek relief in a workhouse.[83]

The Society's prediction that the new poor law would affect only a limited number of the poor was proved correct. According to their annual report of 1840, they claimed that of the 18,000 persons relieved by the Society in 1839-1840, only

6,000 would have been eligible for relief under the new system. While they welcomed this development as lessening some of their burden, their over-riding concern was that unless their funds were maintained at the existing level, even more Roomkeepers would sink into destitution and be driven into the workhouse in search of relief, thereby increasing the burden of the poor-rates. Already there was evidence that contributions were beginning to decline. Between 1837 and 1838 receipts fell by £670. The Society therefore reiterated its appeal to the public to continue to give support.[84]

The anticipated change in attitudes towards relief of the poor following the introduction of statutory poor rates, highlights the role played by charitable organisations in the late eighteenth and early nineteenth centuries. Clearly a 'charitable feeling' towards the poor had become part of the whole ethos of the Society, with a high and sustained level of voluntary participation which is often difficult for us to understand. The Roomkeepers' Society offers several outstanding individual examples of this philanthropy, the most prominent being Samuel Rosborough, a central figure in the Society's work for the first forty years of its existence, who served as treasurer from 1809 onwards. When it was decided in 1830 to open an account in La Touche's bank it was acknowledged to be 'a delicate subject to carry out without hurting the treasurer's feelings'. The respect the Society had for Rosborough was shown after his death in 1832, for a memorial tablet was promptly erected in his honour at Saint Michan's church.[85]

Rosborough had written a pamphlet on the condition of Dublin's poor in 1801 in which he expressed concern for the poor who suffered far from the public eye, in contrast to the street-wise beggars for whom he had little sympathy. His motivation in wishing to help the poor seems to have been the straightforward one of Christian charity, with no regard whatever as to 'their religious prejudices, opinions and professions'.[86] It is also from Rosborough that we can glean some information about another of the founding members of the Society, Laurence Toole, secretary from 1790 until his death in 1817. Toole he said acted as secretary...for four years without fee or reward until, the business of the Society becoming so extensive as to occupy almost the entire of his leisure, he was under the necessity of giving up his profession as a school-master to take upon him that as secretary to this Society.[87]

There were numerous others whose names keep re-appearing among the Society's records about whom almost nothing is known: Archibald Hamilton, an attorney from Jervis Street; Peter Brophy, a merchant on Ormond quay; John Grehan, the carver and gilder from North Anne Street; and Jonathan Hill, a drug merchant from Capel Street. Their motives, and those of the hundreds of ordinary members, remain obscure.

The involvement of several Protestant clergymen in the Society raises the issue of what links, if any, the Society had with the evangelical movement which played such an important role in many charitable organisations in Ireland during the early nineteenth century. One of the clergymen most prominently involved in the Society was the Rev. Joseph Stopford, a Fellow of Trinity College and later rector of Letterkenny, who was Treasurer from 1797 to 1804. We know of Stopford mainly through his influential role as tutor to divinity students in Trinity, in which capacity he brought students on frequent visits to several of Dublin's charities.[88] Stopford was involved in several evangelical societies, including the Hibernian Sunday School Society, and he also had links with Methodism. What we know of his religious convictions suggests that this was not incompatible with membership of the inter-denominational Roomkeepers' Society. The Rev. Peter Roe quotes Stopford as writing, with regard to his views on Christianity: 'we may have strenuous zeal, but if we...have not long-suffering meekness and charity, we have not the Spirit', and the Rev. John Jebb wrote of Stopford's 'charitable and friendly feeling for Christians of all denominations'. A third student who wrote of Stopford, described him more irreverently as 'the perfect curd...of the purest milk of human kindness'.[89]

The other most visible link with the evangelical movement was the inclusion on the committee of trustees in 1796 of the Rev. John Walker, another Trinity College Fellow, but one whose evangelical involvement was much more pronounced. In the 1790s Walker was still an Anglican, but his controversial theological opinions later led to his expulsion from Trinity and his founding of an extreme Calvinist sect in 1805.[90] It is likely that Walker's involvement in the Roomkeepers' Society was fairly peripheral as he is not mentioned in the Society's records after 1796. Another of the Fellows of Trinity at this time numbered among the Society's trustees had a more practical involvement: the physician, Whitley Stokes, also held unorthodox political and religious opinions; he was a friend of Theobald Wolfe Tone, who described him as 'the very best man I have ever known', and he had been a member of the Dublin United Irish Society in its strictly constitutional phase. He later opposed revolutionary methods to effect political change because of what Tone described as 'his extravagant anxiety for the lives of others'.[91] Stokes' humanitarianism in his treatment of disease among Dublin's poor has been well documented[92] and although he was sympathetic to the Calvanist beliefs of Walker, his social philosophy was based on the same principle of tolerance for all denominations on which the Roomkeepers' Society had been founded.[93]

The links with evangelicalism are therefore tenuous, yet the religious motivation of the activists in the Society seems clear. Another motivating factor, which was often explicit in their appeals to the public, was the utilitarian value of the Society as an agency for discouraging begging in the streets. Graves' sermon in 1797 illustrates this: he claimed that the founders, 'conscious that the mendicants who infest our streets almost always extort relief', sought 'to remedy this abuse of public munificence, by directing it to objects truly worthy of its exercise'.[94] The Society itself underlined this aspect of its work in 1830 when they claimed to have been

> essentially instrumental in preventing the increase of mendicancy, by conveying relief to the distressed tradesmen and the reduced citizen at their own dwellings, and thereby limiting the growth of pauperism.

This preoccupation with the prevention of street begging seems more often aimed at alleviating the discomfort of those who had to witness the 'public exhibition of human misery with which the inhabitants of this city [are] already too familiar', and at preventing the spread of contagious diseases, rather than at relieving the sufferings of the poor themselves.[95] It must be remembered however that the Roomkeepers' were here appealing for continued financial support and, perhaps inevitably, they directed the public's attention towards the practical benefits which resulted from their work.

The Society, like many other charitable bodies at the time, operated with relative anonymity and little material benefit to its members. It filled the vacuum of poor relief in Dublin city in a period when parliament's response to the problem was so obviously inadequate. The need for such an institution was clear from the public response to its establishment and from its rapid growth in the early years. It is significant that the Society's basis of support remained throughout this era among the manufacturers and artisans of Dublin, which were the groups with which the Roomkeepers' Society's relief programme was primarily concerned. Yet the motivation of the active members of the Society, the officers, and the ordinary divisional inspectors, and their enormous investment of time and effort, cannot be understood in terms of practical social action. The explanation seems to lie in the Christian ethos of the day and in this respect the Roomkeepers' Society was unique in its strict adherence to the inter-denominational principle, expressed in a motto used by the Society in 1797: 'bout faith and hope the world may disagree, but all mankind's concern is Charity'.[96] The perseverance of the activists of the Society, in face of the numerous and varied obstacles to their work, and their success in supplying a minimum level of relief for hundreds of their poorer peers in the city, testifies to their dedication to an essentially humane philosophy derived from the Enlightenment.

NOTES

1.   J.Warburton, J.Whitelaw, and R.Walsh, *History of the City of Dublin* (1818) I, 169-170.
2.   *Dublin Gazette,* 6 July 1822.

3. C.E. Maxwell, *Dublin under the Georges* (1956) pp.141-3.
4. Warburton, op. cit. II, p.900.
5. Sick and Indigent Roomkeepers' Society records in Public Record Office (henceforth 'SIRS') 1028/3/1; SIRS, 1028/4/2; *Poor Enquiry (Ireland)*, App.C, Part II: *Report on the City of Dublin*, (Brit. Parl. Papers, 1836), xxx, (henceforth *Poor Enquiry*), p.227; M.J. Tutty, 'Dublin's Oldest Charity', *Dub. Hist. Rec.*, XVI, 3, (March, 1961), 73-74.
6. SIRS, 1028/3/1, 11.
7. SIRS, 1028/4/2, 22 .
8. SIRS, 1028/4/3, 'Receipts and Expenditure, with families and persons relieved from the commencement in 1790, to the present year 1888'.
9. SIRS, 1028/4/3; Warburton, op. cit., p.900.
10. SIRS, 1028/3/1.
11. SIRS, 1028/4/2; *Dublin Journal*, 17 December, 1799.
12. For example, Mr. Joseph Goff's inspection, SIRS, 1028/4/2, 4 January, 1805.
13. SIRS, 1028/3/1, 11 August, 1799.
14. SIRS 1028/3/1, 11 March, 1797.
15. Ibid.
16. SIRS 1028/3/1, 11 April, 1800.
17. SIRS 1028/3/1, note inserted after entry for 14 November, 1800.
18. SIRS 1028/3/1, 2 November, 1827.
19. SIRS 1028/1/1, Printed Annual Report ('AR') 1828.
20. SIRS 1028/1/3, AR 1839.
21. *Poor Enquiry*, p.226.
22. SIRS 1028/3/1, 4 April, 1806.
23. For example, SIRS 1028/3/1, 5 March, 1819.
24. SIRS 1028/4/2/.
25. Maxwell, op. cit. p.171.
26. SIRS 1028/4/2.
27. SIRS 1028/1/1, AR 1823.
28. SIRS 1028/4/2.
29. Ibid.
30. Ibid.
31. SIRS 1028/4/3.
32. *Dublin Journal*, 17 November, 1799.
33. SIRS 1028/4/2, 6 July, 1832.
34. SIRS 1028/4/3.
35. SIRS 1028/3/1, 11 December, 1800.

36. Ibid., 21 Februrary, 1817.
37. SIRS 1028/4/1, 22 September, 1828.
38. SIRS 1028/3/1, 28 February, 1817.
39. SIRS 1028/3/1, 6 February, 1801.
40. *Poor Enquiry*, op. cit. p.241.
41. Ibid. p.228.
42. SIRS 1028/3/1, 11 April, 1800.
43. Samuel Rosborough, *Observations on the State of the Poor of the Metrropolis...* (Dublin, 1801), p.35.
44. SIRS 1028/3/1, 12 January, 1798.
45. SIRS 1028/4/2, 1 April, 1803.
46. *Dublin Journal*, 20 January, 1798.
47. SIRS 1028/3/1, 3 July, 1801; SIRS 1028/1/1, AR 1823 pp.7-8.
48. Richard Graves, *A Sermon in aid of the United Charitable Society for the Relief of Indigent Roomkeepers, Saint Werburgh's Church, February 21 1796* (Dublin 1796), p.21; Whitley Stokes, *Projects for Reestablishing the Internal Peace and Tranquility of Ireland* (Dublin, 1799), p.34.
49. *Poor Enquiry*, op. cit. submissions by Charles Sharpe, Micheal Carroll and John Murray, pp.232, 233, 235.
50. SIRS 1028/1/1, AR 1826, p.6; AR 1829, p.8.
51. Stokes, op. cit. p.39; Tutty, op. cit. p.81.
52. SIRS 1028/1/1, AR 1823, p.7.
53. Ibid.
54. *Poor Enquiry*, op. cit. pp.230-231, see also evidence of T.J.Delahunt, p.232; and Peter Mackin, p.233.
55. SIRS 1028/4/3.
56. SIRS 1028/4/3.
57. *Watson's Almanack* (Dublin, 1797), pp.141-142.
58. SIRS 1028/4/2, accounts for the years 1796 and 1797.
59. SIRS 1028/1/1, AR 1823, pp.21-35, AR 1828, pp.30-47; SIRS 1028/1/3, AR 1839, pp32-60.
60. *Poor Enquiry*, op. cit. Submission of George Browne, p.232, (also concluding remarks by Commissioners) p.344.
61. Tutty, op. cit. p.74.
62. SIRS 1028/3/1; Tutty, op. cit. p.74; SIRS 1028/4/2.
63. SIRS 1028/3/1.
64. SIRS 1028/1/3, AR 1839, p.71.
65. Tutty, op. cit. p.82.
66. SIRS 1028/4/2, 10 February, 1810; Tutty, op. cit., p.82.

67. *Poor Enquiry*, op. cit., submission of Delahunt, p.231; (concluding observations of Commissioners) p.344.
68. For example SIRS 1028/3/1, 20 February, 1824.
69. SIRS 1028/4/2, 18 February, 1831.
70. Ibid. 12 August, 1831.
71. *Poor Enquiry*, op. cit. p.239.
72. SIRS 1028/4/2, 3 April, 1807.
73. Graves, op. cit. p.13; *Dublin Journal*, January 13 1798.
74. Warburton, op. cit. p.900. SIRS 1028/1/1, AR 1829, p.9.
75. Rosborough, op. cit. pp.40-41.
76. Graves, op. cit. p.13.
77. SIRS, memorandum inserted, 8 March, 1799.
78. For example: SIRS 1028/4/2, 24 June, 1831; 24 February, 1832, 24 June, 1832.
79. SIRS 1028/1/3, AR 1835, p.5.
80. SIRS 1028/4/3, 9 December, 1826.
81. *Dublin Directory* (1834), p.269.
82. SIRS 1028/4/2, 22 April, 1836.
83. SIRS 1028/4/2, 22 April, 1836.
84. Ibid. AR 1838, p.4; AR 1839, p.9.
85. Tutty, op. cit. p.84.
86. Rosborough, op. cit. p.84.
87. Ibid. pp.37-38.
88. Samuel Madden, *Memoir of the Life of Reverend Peter Roe* (Dublin, 1842), pp.29-30.
89. Ibid. p.145; Charles Forster, *Thirty Years' Correspondence between John Jebb and Alexander Knox* pp.10-13; C.E. Maxwell, *History of Trinity College Dublin* (1946), p.260.
90. SIRS 1028/3/1, 10 March, 1797; Maxwell, *History of Trinity,* p.273; T.D.Stubbs, *History of Trinity College* (1899), pp.311-2.
91. W.Tone, (ed.) *Life of Theobald Wolfe Tone* (Washington, 1826), 1, 40-42.
92. *Dublin University Magazine* (August 1845), 202-210.
93. Stubbs, op. cit. p.143; Stokes, op. cit. pp.44-45.
94. Graves, op. cit. p.8.
95. SIRS 1028/1/1, AR 1830, p.4; SIRS 1028/1/3, AR 1835, p.3, 10.
96. Graves, op. cit. p.34.

THE EMPLOYMENT CRISIS
OF 1826

DAVID O'TOOLE

Dublin was a great bee-hive of craft industries in the eighteenth century, most of which depended on the home market for their prosperity. Among them, the handicraft weaving of fine woollen and silk was the most important, giving employment to thousands of weavers and many more ancillary workers in the older quarters of the city. These textile workers were always at the mercy of a fickle market; every decade saw a bad year or two when the living standards of the otherwise well-to-do artisans fell, forcing many of them to depend on charity. But for most of the century, the textile industries were a dynamo for the capital's economy.

By the beginning of the nineteenth century things were changing. The weaving of cotton and various types of mixed fabric was now much more important; weaving skills were more easily learnt, and wages in real terms were slipping back; the old workshop structure of production was now being undermined by the emergence of a few large-scale employers who were often involved in the new mechanical technology - out-of-town spinning mills and suburban textile printing yards. A more fundamental threat to employment came from the growing sophistication of the cross-channel textile industry. The spectacular fall in the production costs of cotton and the competitive climate this created threatened all textile manufactures, even the cotton industry, in all but the most cost-effective locations.

The exposed position of Dublin's textile industry was revealed in two ways: by the gradual long-term decline in the standard of living of city textile workers as employers squeezed costs to remain competitive; and by the sudden catastrophic waves of industrial bankruptcy and unemployment that came in the wake of business slumps in Britain when, among other things, textiles were dumped on the Irish market at knock-down prices by English manufacturers desperate to liquidate stocks quickly. One such shock, coming in the middle years of Napoleonic prosperity, was in 1809-10; this seems to have halted growth in most of the newer branches of textile manufactures in the neighbourhood of Dublin. More devastating in its effects was the 1826 slump.[1] The catalyst for this was the monetary crisis in England in December 1825 when sixty-six banks suspended payments for one week.[2] The price of cotton collapsed, and many industries within the textile trade found themselves in difficulty. Irish manufacturers suffered doubly because of, once again, the dumping of goods by English businesses; this expedient was now all the more attractive for them because they had duty-free access to the Irish market, thanks to the removal of the final tariff barriers in Anglo-Irish trade in 1824.

The economic slump of 1826 in Ireland seems to have had a permanently devastating effect on urban textile manufacturing in southern Irish towns,[3] but the impact on Dublin was sensational. By the summer of that year over 3,100 looms were idle and some 20,000 people (10 per cent of the population of the city) were directly affected by the collapse in employment;[4] the majority of these were by then dependent on some form of public relief. These facts have been highlighted by others, but in discussing the plight of the Dublin weavers, historians have confined themselves to the chronology of the collapse and the general economic context. The aim here is to pin-point the location of those who had been employed in the city textile trade and who were now in distress; to examine the extent to which the textile industry was permanently wiped out within Dublin; and thirdly, to speculate as to the reason for the failure of the textile industry to bounce back after 1826.

The Dublin textile industry has always been conventionally linked with the south-western Liberties, but was the weaving population restricted to the Liberties, and did those who were distressed in 1826 come exclusively from this one area of the city? Two sources help to answer these questions: (i) accounts kept of persons employed in emergency relief work during 1826, and (ii) lists of persons receiving charitable food donations. Both these activities were organised by the Paving Board and the secretariat in Dublin Castle (although most of the funds came from private donations, not from the exchequer). The 'Labourers Accounts' detail the payments made to 'tradesmen of the manufacturing class' employed in road-repairing and stone-breaking in the city and suburbs. Each account recorded the name of the labourer, his address, age, previous occupation, number of days employed, and the number of family members. From these lists, data on 1,522 names were assembled,[5] nearly all of whom were textile operatives (see Table I). The lists of 'Food Recipients' were derived from a large number of rather smaller accounts, each account containing a bundle of tickets entitling the holder to a certain amount of potatoes and oatmeal. From these accounts, data on 1,004 names were assembled.[6] Persons listed on the food tickets had only their names and addresses recorded, so without occupational data it has been impossible to determine whether or not those recipients were predominantly weavers. However the majority of those receiving food tickets were women, and those listed on the 'Labourers Accounts' were exclusively men.[7] One might therefore assume that the food recipients were the wives of the road-workers, but from an initial comparison of the two sets of names there is little evidence to support this.

In Map A the addresses of those named on the 'Labourers Accounts' have been plotted, in Map B the addresses of those receiving food tickets. The pattern in Map A indicates a great concentration of weavers situated in the area of the Liberties. The majority of addresses were in the adjoining parishes of St. Luke's and St. Catherine's, including such overpopulated streets as the Coombe, Newmarket, Pimlico, Pool St., Cork St., and Marrowbone Lane. Outside the boundaries of the Earl of Meath's Liberties, the only parishes with a large weaving

MAP A

Location of Weavers employed on Public Works, 1826

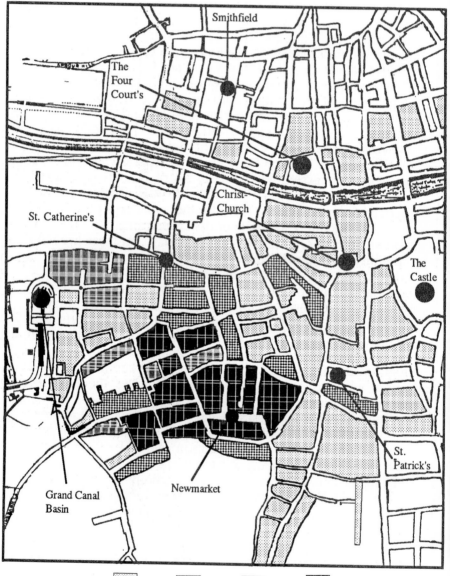

MAP B

Location of Food Recipients, 1826

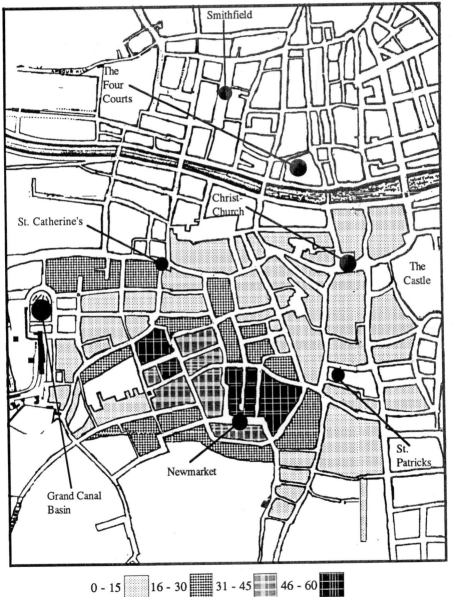

0 - 15   16 - 30   31 - 45   46 - 60

population were, it seems, St. Nicholas' Without, around Ash
St. and Spitalfields, and St. Patrick's Deanery around New St.
and Kevin St. These two parishes are of course close to the
Liberties' boundaries.[8] The striking thing about the distribution
in St. Nicholas' Without is the relatively low percentage of
weavers around Francis St., a street traditionally associated
with drapers, clothiers and mercers - the master-manufacturers
and middlemen of the previous century. Smaller concentrations
of weavers are evident in the areas of St. Bride's, near Golden
Lane, St. Audeon's around Cook St. and High St. and north of
the river in St. Michan's around Church St. West of the city,
small weaving communities appear in the Bowbridge area at
Kilmainham and at Islandbridge where there was a major textile
printing works. Other areas outside the city where weavers
were located include Ballsbridge, Harold's Cross,
Whitechurch, Palmerstown and Chapelizod. All these areas had
water-powered cotton mills, printing works, or both, and one
would expect cotton weavers to be living close to such sites.[9]
Most of the weavers listed in the accounts worked on the road-
schemes near Bowbridge, Kings Inn St. and Harold's Cross.[10]
Just how badly affected the weavers must have been is
indicated by the fact that some of those employed in the road-
repairing schemes walked from as far as Celbridge, Co.
Kildare, thirteen miles from the city.

The groups of workers employed on the relief schemes
were placed under the control of an overseer, who in most
cases had himself been involved in the textile trade and who
lived in the same general area as the workers employed under
him. Possibly the overseers were displaced masters, and the
road workers wage-earning journeymen. The rationale behind
using overseers to organise the distribution of work amongst
the weavers was obvious: since the overseers were textile
people, they would have some knowledge of the individual
workers; this ensured that the employment given was
effeciently distributed and organised, and that work was only
given to *bona fide* industrial workers.

From a sample of 122 names taken from the 'Labourers
Accounts' dated 1 July 1826, the average number of weeks that

'Dutch Billies ' in Sweeney's Lane, St. Luke's Parish, 1913 (Royal Society of Antiquaries of Ireland Coll.).

TABLE 1

Breakdown of Occupations of Persons on Relief Work, 1826

	No.	Per cent
Cotton Weavers	433	29.0
Silk Weavers	181	12.1
Broad Cloth Weavers	219	14.6
Linen Weavers	12	0.8
Other Weavers	227	15.2
Dyers (Woollen & Cotton)	63	4.2
Spinners	113	7.6
Shearsmen	39	2.1
Cutters	19	1.3
Others (Printers, Hosiers,Tanners, etc.)	189	11.6
Total with occupations recorded	1495	12.6

Source: 'Labourers on Account' (1826), (State Paper Office, OP/588t/727); 'List of Food Recipients on Public Account', (State Paper Office, OP/588s/726).

each labourer was employed was 15.3 weeks, while from accounts dated 29 August from a sample of 44 names, the average was 10.8 weeks. This suggests that despite a good initial provision of relief employment, by late summer when a typhus fever epidemic was at its worst, funds were less readily available for the provision of employment by the Relief Committee to those in distress. This thesis is supported by an analysis of the amounts paid to those on the relief schemes. In the returns of men employed on 3 June and 9 June, ordinary labourers were paid 1s.0d. per day and each overseer was paid 1s.6d. But in the 'Return of the Men Employed upon the Road Leading from Bowbridge to Kilmainham, commencing Monday, 28 August and ending 21 September, 1826',[11] all workers employed were paid 6d. per day with an additional 1d.

paid for each dependant in the worker's family. Each overseer was paid 1s. Either the flow of voluntary funds for the payment of the workers had decreased drastically, or else the numbers of weavers made redundant became so great that the road workers had to be paid less in order to provide something for all seeking employment.

The comparison of those receiving food tickets on relief (Map B) with the weavers (Map A) shows a striking territorial similarity, and confirms that the Liberties were indeed the worst affected area in Dublin in 1826; it is unlikely that those who appear on Map B, while of different families from the road-workers, were also part of the textile community in this area. On closer inspection, Map B shows an even greater concentration of people living within the Liberties: those living in the area of the Coombe, Skinners' Alley, Fordham's Alley and Newmarket accounted for 15.25 per cent of the total number of weavers in the 'Labourers Accounts', but formed 28 per cent of the total of those receiving food relief.[12] There was almost no one receiving food relief north of the river and indeed the only areas apart from the parishes of St. Nicholas' Without, St. Bride's and St. Patrick's where food relief was being given were Harold's Cross and Kilmainham. Territorial correlation is less evident in the outlying Dublin districts such as Chapelizod, Palmerstown, Islandbridge and Whitechurch. Nobody with addresses in these areas, or in nearby Celbridge, appears on any of the food tickets.

An analysis of the maps suggests three main points: first, the parishes of St. Catherine's and St. Luke's beyond any doubt comprised the main area of intensive textile activity that suffered during the 1826 collapse; secondly, that in the textile communities around Palmerstown, Chapelizod and Whitechurch, the non-appearance of people from these areas receiving food relief would suggest that outlying districts were less affected by the distress and may have had other forms of employment to resort to in times of need, such as agricultural labour, whereas the Liberties area could offer no alternative employment when the textile industry withered away in 1826; thirdly, the fact that many of those people receiving food in the

Liberties were not related to publicly employed weavers
suggests that the impact of 1826 was felt brutally by all types
of worker in the affected neighbourhoods.

* * *

These public-relief schemes were part of the Royal
Exchange Relief Committee's efforts to relieve distress in the
city. The committee was a voluntary relief organisation that had
been established in the Weavers' Hall in the Coombe; it merged
with the larger relief committee set up by Rev. Edward Groves
under the chairmanship of the Lord Mayor.[13] By August 1826
the committee had collected £8,431, some of it from England
including a donation from the King, and of this, £5,147 was
used to pay the poor employed on road and other relief works,
£1,404 was given in gratuitous relief to the sick and feeble, and
£227 was given to the Paving Board for miscellaneous works
carried out to aid the poor. Most of the government aid in 1826
was allocated to district relief bodies and a total of £3,700 was
spent.[14]

The unprecedented urban relief schemes were not enough to
avert a public health crisis. By September 1826 the number of
hospitalised fever patients was four times greater than in April,
when the full extent of the crisis had yet to be felt; altogether,
5,000 people sick of fever, including those confined at home,
were reported.[15] To make matters worse, hospitals were quite
inadequate and although the House of Industry offered some
relief to the poor, the lack of a full poor-law system meant that
the city was ill-equipped to deal with major health crises.
Hospitals were overcrowded, and this necessitated the erection
of temporary shelters and tents for the sick, most of them close
to the Cork St. hospital on the edge of the Liberties. By
September there were seven hospitals receiving fever patients;
the Meath, Whitworth, Kevin St., the House of Recovery in
Cork St., the Hardwicke Fever (an extension of the House of
Industry), Sir Patrick Dun's and Dr. Steeven's. Of the 5,000
who were infected, approximately 1,400 were being cared for
in the hospitals. This figure remained steady for some months

and in November there were still 1,362 patients in the Dublin hospitals. By the following May when the fever began to abate, 775 people were still hospitalised.

The total amount of money spent by the government in combatting the epidemic between September 1826 and the following March was in the region of £25,000 to £30,000.[16] This sum was used mainly in hospitals in Dublin but even with this amount the government was only catering for a quarter of those affected with disease. The mortality rate is much harder to assess. Figures for those who died in hospital between September and May indicate a rate of one dead in every twenty-five patients hospitalised, but official report figures indicated that twice as many died overall.[17] The number of patients admitted to Cork St. Hospital in the whole of 1826 was 10,612, while the number of deaths was 380.[18] This represents a death rate of one in every twenty-eight hospitalised. However conditions for those who were sick and were not cared for within the hospitals must have been terrible, and there is no doubt that a higher proportion of those outside died. It has been suggested that the overall excess mortality in the city may well have been over 4,000.[19]

The Dublin weaving community therefore suffered a traumatic year. Many weavers were unable to seek alternative employment and emigrated to places such as Macclesfield and Manchester in England. Some returned to the loom at home however, although it is not clear what proportion did so. The Poor Law Commission of 1838 stated that weavers were then one-third to one-quarter their former number.[20] To what extent therefore, was this official figure an accurate assessment of those weavers who were still active in Dublin in the 1830s?

An initial indication of the extent of individual decline is apparent from a comparison of the 1821 and the 1841 census for the worst affected areas in 1826, St. Catherine's, St. Luke's and St. Nicholas' Without.[21] Although there was a population increase of 6.9 per cent in the city between 1821 and 1841 the number of families who were employed in manufacturing industries, trades and handicrafts decreased by 58.5 per cent. The three most intensive weaving parishes all show a decrease in manufacturing industries of 50.6 per cent, 71.5 per cent and 62.1 per cent respectively. However in those parishes where there was almost no weaving population (e.g. St. Michan's, St. Mark's and St. Audeon's) there was an almost identical drop in the percentage of people who were employed in manufacturing and trade. This implies that the broader decline in crafts was as severe if not quite as melodramatic as in the textile sector - or that the censal occupation data are seriously misleading.

What of the subsequent history of those weavers who had appeared on the relief returns of 1826? From a sample of 643 weavers' names, only two appeared in the 1834 *Dublin Directory*: a silk weaver from Cork St. and a carpet manufacturer from Chamber St. A sample of 443 names taken from those receiving food relief in 1826 yielded slightly more positive results: 17 names reappeared in 1834. An interesting point about these 17 persons is that only five were listed in 1834 under occupations relating to the textile trade. This would confirm the suggestion that many food recipients in 1826 had not then been directly involved in the textile industry. It is unlikely - but not impossible - that weavers would have switched to occupations such as hatters, slaters and pawnbrokers by 1834.

Ten names that appeared in 1826 as food recipients and/or labourers on relief were from the small St. Bride's parish. Alone of city parishes, the full census schedules for 1831 survive;[22] however an examination revealed no evidence of the community of weavers which had existed around the Golden Lane area of the parish in 1826. This is perhaps even more telling evidence than the exercise linking 1826 with the 1834 *Directory*; both sources nonetheless show the extent of the dislocating effects of 1826. Those who found employment in the diminished handicraft industries after 1826 seem to have been different people from the victims of the crash. One contemporary, writing of St. Luke's parish in 1833, claimed that only the silk, tabinet and poplin manufacture survived then, but that 'the young only find employment [in them], that branch of business requiring good sight, and consequently, leaving the aged to seek a precarious mode of existence by mendicancy'.[23]

Why then was there no recovery of cotton, woollen and linen manufacturing around Dublin, no transition to mechanised mill-centred employment as was beginning to occur around Belfast? The fact that the Dublin collapse occured so soon after the removal of tariffs in 1824 has led many to believe that this was the major reason. However the abolition of protective duties was only a small part of the process. Indeed free trade offered new export opportunities to Irish manufacturers and textile printers to break into the lucrative British market.[24] The city textile industry, as we have noted, showed signs of weakness long before the 1826 decline. In the new climate of falling production costs and a widening market for cheaper textiles, ports, capital cities and old high-cost urban centres were inappropriate sites - as the history of Liverpool, London and Norwich showed: all were de-industrialising and so we should not wonder at Dublin following a similar path. By 1826, it is obvious that investment within the Dublin textile industry had become very unattractive. Despite lower labour costs, it offered unattractively low rates of return, and money was increasingly enticed out of textiles into more lucrative enterprises. After the collapse in 1826, there were few investment incentives that might have led to industrial rehabilitation.

In the overall economic context, the changes within the urban economy in the 1820s and 1830s were no less important.The coming of free trade was significant in a wider sense: there is no doubt that the greater integration of the British and Irish consumer and producer markets in the early nineteenth century meant that there was an over-reliance on the part of the Irish manufacturers on domestic and British markets. Free trade was however advantageous to some sectors, especially agriculture, but not to Irish manufacturing - linen and alcohol excepted. Throughout this period there was a shift in the terms of trade in favour of agriculture, for although agricultural prices were falling, their fall was less than that of industrial goods. This change in the whole nature of trade was reflected by the character of trade through Dublin port: industrial exports were quite eclipsed but agricultural exports soared, especially with the new steam-ship services in the 1820s.[25] But all this meant little to the Liberties which was now becoming an urban wasteland, as some emigrated, others grew old in poverty, and buildings were neglected. 1826 was indeed an urban watershed as powerful in its own way as 1847 was in much of rural Ireland.

NOTES

1.   D. Dickson, 'Aspects of the Rise and Decline of the Irish Cotton Industry', in L.M. Cullen and T.C.Smout (eds.) *Comparative Aspects of Scottish and Irish...History* (Edinburgh, 1977), p. 109-110.

2.   T.P. O' Neill, 'The State, Poverty and Distress in Ireland', (unpublished Ph.D. Thesis, University College, Dublin, 1971), p.15.

3.   E.R.R. Green, *The Lagan Valley, 1800-50* (London, 1949), p.102.

4.   *Dublin Evening Post* and *Saunder's Newsletter*, 25 April, 1826. See also *Transactions of College of Physicians,* (cited in Brit. Parl. Papers, 1856, XXIX, p.200).

5.   'Labourers on Account' (1826), (State Paper Office, OP/588t/727), hence-forth (S.P.O. OP/588t/727). The total of 1522 names was derived from a very thorough check.

6.   'List of Food Recipients on Public Account', (S.P.O. OP/588s/726). The sample of 1,004 names represents approx-imately 70-80 per cent of the total number of food tickets. The tickets were all hand-written and some of them are completely illegible.

7.   Some of those cited in the Labourers Accounts included boys aged between 10-16 years.

8.   J.Warburton, J.Whitelaw, R.Walsh, *History of the City of Dublin* (Lon-don, 1818), I, ch.5.

9.   Ibid., p. 976 (Lists of Cotton Mills in Dublin around 1816-18).

10.   'Labourers on Account', op. cit. Most account lists give the area where road works were in operation.

11.   'Labourers on Account', op. cit.

12. These percentage totals are derived from a breakdown of the total number of people living in each street.

13. T. O' Neill, 'A Bad Year in the Liberties', in E. Gillespie (ed.)*The Liberties of Dublin* (Dublin, 1972), p. 79.

14. O' Neill does not state when this money was given or how much of it was given to the Relief Exchange Committee.

15. 'Report of Managing Committee of Cork Street Hospital, 1826', in *Brit. Parl. Papers,* 1856, XXIX, pp. 205, 467.

16. Goulburn said that the Government was spending £120 per day combatting urban fever: cited in O'Neill (1971), op. cit., p.170.

17. Ibid., p.172.

18. 'Report of Managing Committee of Cork Street Hospital', op. cit., pp. 201, 465.

19. O'Neill, (1971), op. cit., p. 173.

20. L.M. Cullen, *An Economic History of Ireland since 1660,* (London,1972), p. 120.

21. *Census of Ireland, 1821 & 1841* (Brit. Parl. Papers, 1824, XXII; 1843 XXIV).

22. 1831 Census of St. Bride's Parish (National Library P-1994).

23. F. White, *Report and Observations on the State of the Poor of Dublin* (Dublin, 1833), p.13.

24. Dickson, (1977), op. cit., p. 110.

25. Cullen, op. cit., p.109.

BIBLIOGRAPHICAL NOTE

Three great publications of the last century are still valuable, for reference purposes at least: J. Warburton et al., *History of the City of Dublin*, 2 vols. (London, 1818); J.T. Gilbert's street by street survey, *History of the City of Dublin*, 3 vols. (Dublin, 1854-9; 2nd ed. with index, 1978); and Gilbert's *Calendar of the Ancient Records of Dublin*, 19 vols. (Dublin, 1896-1944), being the full minutes of Dublin Corporation up to 1840.

There have been many general surveys of the city covering this period published in recent decades, of which the best are Constantia Maxwell, *Dublin under the Georges* (London, 1938); Peter Somerville-Large, *Dublin* (Dublin, 1979); and Patrick Fagan, *The Second City...Dublin 1700-60* (Dublin, 1986). The city's architectural history has received more sustained and analytical treatment than any other aspect; Maurice Craig's *Dublin 1660-1860: A Social and Architectural History* (London, 1952); C.P. Curran's *Dublin Decorative Plasterwork in the 17th and 18th Centuries* (London, 1967); and Edward McParland's *James Gandon:Vitruvius Hibernicus* (London, 1985) are excellent studies, more wide-ranging than any of the other monographs on the city at this period.

Many articles relating to architecture, planning and the building trade have appeared in the *Bulletin of the Irish Georgian Society*, but some of the most interesting research in the area (e.g. by Nuala Burke) remains in unpublished theses. On the history of labour and employment, a few articles and some excellent unpublished work (e.g. by Fergus D'Arcy) do not fill a major gap. On trade and commerce, the most helpful books are those by L.M. Cullen, *Princes and Pirates: The Dublin Chamber of Commerce 1783-1983* (Dublin, 1983) and the book of essays, five of which relate to Dublin, edited by Paul Butel and L.M. Cullen, *Cities and Merchants: French and Irish Perspectives on Urban Development 1500-1900* (Dublin, 1986). On financial history, see W.A. Thomas' *The Stock Exchanges of Ireland* (Liverpool, 1986), and F.S.L. Lyons (ed.), *The Bank of Ireland: Bicentenary Essays* (Dublin, 1983).

Industrial history has been less well served, outside of drink and publishing. The most useful in the latter areas are: P. Lynch and J. Vaizey, *Guinness's Brewery and the Irish Economy 1759-1876* (Cambridge, 1960); Robert Munter, *History of the Irish Newspaper 1685-1760* (Cambridge, 1967), and R.C. Cole, *Irish Booksellers and English Writers 1730-1800* (London, 1986).

No full study as yet exists on the topic of Dublin municipal politics, but see Sean Murphy's 'The Corporation of Dublin 1660-1760', in *Dublin Historical Record*, XXXVIII (1984-5), and Jacqueline Hill's 'The Politics of Privilege: Dublin Corporation and the Catholic Question 1792-1823', in *Maynooth Review*, VII (1982). On religion in the city, see in particular Nuala Burke's 'A Hidden Church?', in *Archivium Hibernicum*, XXXII (1974).

Upper-class social life is well documented, that of the artisans and the unskilled not. For the former, see La Tourette Stockwell, *Dublin Theatres and Theatre Customs 1637-1820* (New York, 1938) and Ian C. Ross (ed.), *Public Virtue, Public Love....*(Dublin, 1986).

Public health, demography and social structure have been the subject of many theses and articles, but little has been presented in an accessible form. See however William Doolin, *The Dublin Surgeon-Anatomists* (Dublin, 1987), Joseph Robins' *The Lost Children* and *Fools and Mad: A History of the Insane in Ireland* (Dublin, 1980 and 1986).

For these and many other facets of Dublin's history in this period, see also the *Dublin Historical Record* which for nearly 50 years has appeared quarterly.

INDEX